LONGMAN KEY SKILLS

LEVEL 3

WWO • LP • PS

Barry Smith

Longman

Longman Key Skills
titles available in the series

Application of Number Level 1+2
Application of Number Level 3

Communication Level 1+2
Communication Level 3

Information Technology Level 1+2
Information Technology Level 3

Working with Others (WWO)/Improving Own Learning and Performance (LP)/
Problem Solving (PS) Level 1+2

Working with Others (WWO)/Improving Own Learning and Performance (LP)/
Problem Solving (PS) Level 3

Pearson Education Limited
Edinburgh Gate, Harlow
Essex CM20 2JE, England
and Associated Companies throughout the world

First published 2001

British Library Cataloguing in Publication Data
A catalogue entry for this title is available from the British Library

ISBN 0-582-43219-7

Set by 3 in Sabon and Quay Sans
Printed in Great Britain by Henry Ling Ltd
at the Dorset Press, Dorchester, Dorset

Contents

Art and Design • Business • Construction and the Built Environment • Design
and Technology • Engineering • General Studies • Geography • Health and
Social Care • History • Hospitality and Catering • Information and
Communication Technology • Land and Environment • Leisure and Recreation •
Manufacturing • Mathematics • Media • Modern Foreign Languages •
Performing Arts • Retail and Distributive Services • Science • Travel and Tourism

How to use this book

This book helps you obtain the three key skills required at level 3: 'Working with others', 'Improving own learning and performance' and 'Problem solving'. Whether you will be doing your key skills with your other studies in a school, college or at work, this book will help you gain the knowledge, skills and understanding you need to achieve the key skills. This book also offers advice on how to tackle the evidence requirements of the three key skills and indicates where you could look to generate evidence.

The good news about gaining any of the key skills is that you don't always need to do extra work. The evidence for the key skill can be produced while you are doing your normal study and work in the classroom, laboratory, workshop, while at work or even at play.

You can use this book in different ways, it depends on your need. For example, you might not need to read it from the beginning, you may be comfortable with the learning requirements for a particular key skill but need help with the evidence requirements. In this case, Parts 2 and 3 will be most useful. To get the most out of this book, have a look at the following summary of how it is organised and decide how you can use it best.

Part 1: The Learning Curve

This part of the book concentrates on what you need to know to get the key skill units. It has useful information about how to plan and evaluate your work, how to work effectively with other people and how to solve problems. This part looks at the knowledge, skills and understanding for all three key skills together because there is a relationship between some of the content in the key skills. For example, there are parts of planning and evaluating that relate to all three key skills.

Part 2: The Bottom Line

This part of the book tells you what you must do to gain the key skills units. It explains:

- The words and ideas of the key skills
- What is expected at level 3
- What must be in your portfolio of evidence

Part 3: Opportunities

This part of the book is split into two sections. The first section shows you where to find opportunities to create key skill evidence in the courses or qualifications you may be taking. Rather than looking at particular qualifications, this section looks at subject areas and the type of topics they would normally contain which could be used to generate key skill evidence for each of the three key skills.

The second section looks at opportunities to generate evidence for each of the three key skills using non-course-related activities.

Margin

Look in the margin for simple explanations of important words and ideas.

Part 1: The Learning Curve

This part of the book shows you what you need to know to gain your key skills qualification. It deals with the knowledge, skills and understanding involved in planning, implementing and reviewing work. This will be useful for all of the key skills covered in this book.

This part is divided into five sections:

- Take charge of your learning
- Planning
- Reviewing and evaluating
- Group work
- Problem solving
- Using the Internet

Take charge of your learning

The learning zone

Spend a little time thinking about how you learn and how you stay motivated. This means looking at your learning environment, recognising what
the obstacles are to your learning, acknowledging what seems to work for
you and what doesn't. How you organise your learning time is also
important. Organising and planning your learning and your work provide
the key to success when you do key skills like 'Working with others',
'Improving own learning and performance', and 'Problem solving'.

Be aware of your own strengths and weaknesses. When you feel that
you have been working well, identify what it was that enabled you to get
on with your work. On the other hand, make a list of things that have
acted as barriers to your progress and recognise them when they come into
play. These could be:

- Noise
- Distractions
- Interruptions
- Tiredness
- Confusion

Each of the three key skills covered in this book is trying to encourage you
to develop as a learner and get you to think about how you relate to your
learning. In the past your learning may have been more about learning
subject content that was organised and prepared for you by others.

The key skills are trying to get you to take more responsibility for your
work and your learning. They encourage you to take control of your own
learning, taking responsibility for planning the work and evaluating it,
pulling together the resources you need and asking advice when you need
to. In this sense, each of the key skills can be useful preparation for higher
education. In the higher education environment you will be expected to
take control of and responsibility for your own work.

Your learning environment

First of all address *where* you will work and look at the pros and cons of
this location as a learning environment. Of course, you will be learning in
a number of locations, for example classrooms, workshops, and your
workplace. This section is really talking about the place you can go to,

that perhaps you can control or organise to suit you. This is a safe learning space where you can go and spend time:

- Reflecting on what you have learned elsewhere
- Organising your thoughts on what you have learned
- Sorting your work, pulling things together
- Spending some quality time focused on your work

Where is your safe space? Your workspace needs to be free of distractions or interruption and somewhere that you can spend some time dedicated to your work. This could be a local library, a part of the school, college or workplace, or your own space at home. You need to identify what places are available to you and then assess which will be the best to use as a quiet learning zone.

If your bedroom is the only place available, get yourself a 'Do not disturb' sign or let people know when you want to work undisturbed. Devote time to your work and use it for work; don't use the time searching for notes, trying to find where you left off the last time you were working or getting ready to work. Manage your space and time so that you can use both effectively.

Next think about *when* you will work. You will need to identify the times of day or the slots in the week that you can set aside and dedicate to your key skills work. This means looking at the other commitments that must be taken care of and identifying when you can find time to dedicate to your key skills work. Careful planning should help you deal with other commitments or obligations and show how conflicting demands are managed and resolved.

Your other demands could be family commitments, social or leisure engagements, and other course demands or employment requirements. You need to factor these into your personal planning process and make sure that these are not so much competing objectives or commitments as running parallel to your key skill work. Set up a 'friendly' schedule to do your key skills work. Don't deprive yourself of the activities that you like doing. This includes watching your favourite television programmes. Work these into your learning schedule as rewards.

You will find that shorter bursts of dedicated activity with sensible breaks in between are the best and most productive way to work. Don't spend long stretches of time struggling over a particular issue. It can be more productive to leave a problem area and move on to something else. Come back to it with a fresh pair of eyes and it might be less of a problem.

Then look at *how* you will work. Careful planning, the ability to see problems and clashes well before they occur, and sensible time management are all important. Other work commitments, demands and activities can be used as a useful way of unwinding and can help to keep you motivated.

Manage your time by setting clear priorities to ensure that you can achieve them. You can use a SWOT analysis or spider diagrams to help you (more on these later). For example, a SWOT analysis can be useful in helping you to evaluate your learning methods.

By setting yourself short-term targets you can apply your efforts

thoroughly to achieving your goal and build on your achievements. Make sure that your targets are sensible and realistic and, above all, measurable so that you know precisely what you have achieved and can reflect on how far you have progressed. By rewarding yourself with strategic breaks after reaching a specific target, you can then return to your studies refreshed and still motivated for the next stage.

Planning

Why have plans in the first place?

A plan serves as a framework for a project and is a useful reference point for everyone involved. It enables you to judge your progress at any time and helps steer you towards your targets. If kept up to date and amended properly, it can serve as a record of events. In terms of the demands of the key skills unit, it will provide a useful record of your intentions for your portfolio of evidence.

The ability to plan is a transferable skill, which means that once you can plan effectively, you will be able to use it in many different aspects of your studies or work. Regardless of context, planning effectively will let you confront challenges in a well thought out and controlled manner.

People think that planning can be a waste of time that prevents them from getting on with the work. Planning actually saves time by focusing your efforts in more productive ways, cutting down on mistakes and wrong decisions that you could make. Planning helps you to prepare for what you need to do, and prepare for unexpected difficulties. This could end up saving you time.

Getting started

There are two important stages you need to consider before you start. Both stages refer to what you will be doing though both have different levels of detail. The first stage deals with your whole activity in general terms; the second stage looks at the specific detail of what you will be doing. The first stage is establishing your *aim*, sometimes called your *goal*. Your aim should describe in uncomplicated language what you would be trying to achieve.

The second stage adds a layer of detail and is far more specific. It deals with the objectives you will need to meet if you are to achieve your aim. Normally people talk about 'aims and objectives' when describing the two levels of detail; however, sometimes this next level of detail can also be referred to as a target rather than an objective, especially when time is involved. This stage looks at the processes involved in setting clear and feasible aims as well as appropriate and measurable targets or objectives.

'Working with others' refers to objectives, while 'Improving own learning and performance' refers to targets

Having a clear aim is useful for focusing brainstorming sessions and will allow you to create spider diagrams and mind maps

Though the key skills don't mention aims or goals as such, you will find that establishing your aims is a useful first step that will help you to:

- Communicate to others your intentions
- Remain focused on what it is you are trying to do
- Set your plan in context
- Use other techniques to explore the challenges ahead

Defining your aims

To define your aims, it helps to have a clear understanding of what you want to accomplish. The aim should be a well-defined statement of what you are trying to do. You should also give an idea of the overall time constraints and an indication of the types of resources you will need. You could also include a description of how you will know when you have achieved your aim. These statements can be made in broad terms because you will break them down into more detail later.

Identify early on who needs to see your aims, timelines and potential lists of resource needs. This allows others to let you know if your project is unmanageable before you get too involved in the work.

People often neglect this part of planning because they think they understand what needs to be done and just want to get on with it. However, not taking time to think things through properly can mean running into difficulty later. You will lose the benefit of sharing your ideas with others and lose their input if you charge on with the work. You will also be missing out on opportunities to create valuable portfolio evidence to show that you have thought through your work properly.

Setting group aims

When you work with a group of people it is important to have everyone contributing to the aims. This will help each member to feel that he or she is part of the team and encourage everyone to take ownership of the work that has to be done. It also helps to start the process of working co-operatively and reinforces the need for joint effort.

Why have objectives or targets?

Aims are fine for recording your broad intentions. They are a clear way of letting others know what you will be doing overall. However, they are too general to implement as a useful plan because they lack detail. Your aim is too general to allow you to work out exactly what resources you will need, what tasks you need to do and how long everything will take. The aim doesn't really tell you much about the sequence of tasks either. This is why you need to break it down into more detail. By breaking your aim down into a series of precise objectives or targets you can make better judgements about what resources you will need, what needs to be done first and how long different activities should take. This will give you the information you need to produce a clear and detailed plan that will be easy to follow, monitor and evaluate.

Setting objectives and targets

It is only when you break your aims down into smaller targets that you begin to get a real impression of the work that will be involved, the resources you will need and the time it is all likely to take. Targets or objectives are basically your aims broken down into a series of smaller statements that describe more precisely what you need to do. Your aims are broader and general, the targets add a layer of detail and precision to your work and are specific and task related.

Setting targets also gets you to think about the sequence of your work, making you consider what preparation needs to be done before you start the work. This is useful in helping you to organise in your mind an order for your activities. It will also be very useful in helping you to devise and monitor your plan.

There are five key characteristics to consider when identifying targets or objectives:

- Specific
- Measurable
- Achievable
- Realistic
- Time-sensitive

Specific

Try to provide enough detail to prevent any misinterpretation or uncertainty about what you intend to do. One of the main mistakes people make when setting targets is to be too vague. This won't help you when you need to establish how well you've done, so break your aim down into precise, small, measurable targets.

Don't go for sweeping statements of intent like 'Do better in English'. Focus on specific areas, for example, use an aim like 'Improve my grammar', or 'Develop my skills in literary criticism (book reviewing)'.

Measurable

It is always helpful to have tangible evidence of completed targets. Evidence and proof are two very powerful words when doing courses like key skills because assessment is dependent on your being able to demonstrate that you have met the requirements, so work on having targets that can be measured or are easily demonstrated. There are lots of ways to do this.

Build into your plan ways of showing how your work is progressing or what you actually achieved when you reached the end of a stage. Treat this as a cut-off point and try to find some way of recording or acknowledging what you have done. If one target has been to read a chapter of a book about something, once you have reached the end, spend some time writing down from memory what you learned. This will not only record the fact

Brainstorming, spider diagrams and **mapping** are all ways of moving from the general aim to precise targets (see page 14)

The key skills suggest that you set SMART targets, i.e.:
Specific
Measurable
Achievable
Realistic
Time-sensitive

that you actually read the chapter but also give you a clear indication of how much you took in and understood while you were reading it. You can use this to judge whether you need to go back and re-read something or take notes on work you have not understood. Alternatively, if one of your targets has been to use the Internet as a resource, keep evidence to show how you used search engines and could find the information you needed. Your evidence could be printouts of your search results and copies of the information you found.

Achievable and realistic

Always consider whether or not your targets are possible. Be aware of both your own and other people's abilities and limitations. Consider carefully whether you are going to be able to meet the challenge you have set yourself.

A common mistake is to be too ambitious when you set your targets. Before you commit yourself to anything make sure you consider:

- The resources you will need
- The time it will take
- The training or skills you need
- The support or help you will need

Then you can consider:

- If the resources are available to you
- Whether you have enough time
- Whether you have the skills you need or can get the training necessary
- Whether the support is available

Cost factors must also be considered. Remember, although an aim is achievable it may not be feasible because it will cost too much or take too long.

Time-sensitive

Time is a critical factor. Are you going to be able to do what you say you can do within a reasonable time frame? Think carefully about the amount of time you will need to do the work successfully and the amount of time that is available to you. Start to allocate rough timelines to targets and tasks. This should begin to give you an idea of whether or not your proposal will be feasible.

Feasibility study

Before taking your initial ideas much further, it is worth doing a feasibility study to establish whether or not you will actually be able to meet your objective or targets. Carrying out a feasibility study will not only help you to determine whether your ideas are going to work, it will also provide some useful evidence showing that you have thought through your early target setting.

Start by writing up your aim in as much detail as possible, clearly explaining what you intend to do. Then, if you have the time, leave it a day or two, come back to it fresh and evaluate the aim against the five SMART criteria. Draw up a table with two columns and put the positives down one side and the negatives down the other. The table shows an example of a possible layout.

	Positive	*Negative*
Specific		
Measurable		
Achievable		
Realistic		
Time-sensitive		

> ## RECAP
>
> Once you have your general aim, techniques like brainstorming, spider diagrams or mind-mapping can be used to help you create smaller, more precise targets or objectives.
>
> Work up your targets or objectives and put them through the SMART test.
>
> Once you feel confident about your targets or objectives and are clear about how long it could take and the resources you need, you can start putting your plan together.

The plan itself

You need to consider what form your plans will take and how you are going to represent targets, time, decision taking and resources. Flowcharts can be a useful way for outlining the whole process and can also be used to focus on particular targets in detail. This is one useful way of representing the sequence of stages in your plan. However, flowcharts may not be the most effective way to help you to show your timelines.

You can find out more about **flowcharts** on page 17

There are specialist tools that can be useful in dealing with scheduling the start, finish and duration of activities. Gantt charts, for example, depict this process using horizontal activity bars along timelines to show the project deadlines and intended progress. These are best used if a project has several targets that may have interim stages. The Gantt chart will let you see the 'timelines' for your different activities on the same page and could be useful in early detection of critical times when there are a number of different activities on the go at the same time.

Gantt charts can be created in a table format putting time intervals as columns and tasks as separate rows. The projected timelines can then be drawn, based on their start and finish times.

This chart was created using a table function in a word-processing software package. The timelines are illustrated by using a thickened line.

Tasks	Weeks									
	1	2	3	4	5	6	7	8	9	10
Task 1	▬	▬	▬							
Task 2		▬	▬	▬	▬					
Task 3					▬					
Task 4	▬	▬	▬	▬	▬	▬	▬	▬		
Task 5								▬	▬	

Example of a Gantt chart

The Gantt chart can be a useful tool for group activities as it can be a simple way to communicate the extent of the group work and a useful way of tracking targets and progress chasing. Note how you can identify week 5 in the chart as being a busy week with three different tasks going on at the same time. Customise your Gantt chart by adding a symbol to show when you will undertake a review of your progress.

However you choose to produce your plan, and whatever techniques you choose to use, aim to have a general overview sheet and a more specific set of plans detailing each target. The general overview will be useful to explain your activity to others and can communicate significant progress, while the detailed work will be more useful as a working tool. At an individual level, consider using action plan sheets to track your progress.

Action plans are very useful ways to keep track of group and individual work. When you work in a group, everyone can receive the same blank action-planning sheets and be asked to show their own individual targets and responsibilities. Once you have written out your action plan check that it takes you through all the tasks that need to be done in order to achieve your objectives or targets. If you are working in a group you need to make sure that all the action plans fit together and will achieve the group aims or objectives. Group action plans shouldn't conflict with each other or repeat work.

You can organise your action plan either to show the tasks that you need to do in sequence or to show how you prioritise your work with the most important tasks at the top.

The example overleaf – a template for an action plan, showing work priorities – shows the type of action plan you could use, but you are free to design one that is more suited to your work. If you create your own action plan using a computer, put it on a 'landscape' page set-up and make sure you leave enough space for the important details. Consider creating a template that others can use and leave it on a disk that others can access and use. If everyone working on the same project uses the same template,

Action Plan for ... *Put the target or objective here*		Date	
Aim: *Put the overall personal or group aim here*	**Details of target or objective:** *Put a brief explanation of your target or objective here*		
Person/people responsible:	Others involved:		Resources needed:

Priority no:	Action required:	Start date	End date	Evidence or proof of achievement

A simple action plan layout

it will be easier to follow and you will be able to spot conflicts and problem areas more easily when the action plans are compared. Keep in mind that a good action plan:

- Makes reference to the overall purpose (your aim)
- States the target or objective that it relates to
- Includes time to be taken and important deadlines
- Is laid out in a clear and logical manner
- Is updated and amended as changes are made
- Will be dated or have a draft number to show it is the current version

Hint: use the table function in your word-processing software to create an action plan

Your planning can be a combination of action plans, flowcharts and Gantt charts. Each has a different purpose and when used in combination with other planning techniques, a complete picture of everything that needs to be done can be built up.

Planning can be used in a number of different contexts and different types of plan suit different circumstances. For example, strategic planning is used by businesses to help them to meet their broad needs. Strategic plans tend to be long range. Your own detailed day-to-day needs are met by personal planning. Specific tasks or projects use single-use plans for one-off situations, whereas standing plans are used to deal with repetitive tasks or routines.

You will probably be more involved with single-use planning when you work on the key skills.

Changes to your plans

There are two particular ways to prepare for and deal with unforeseen circumstances that risk disrupting your plans. The first involves adopting a *flexible* approach to planning, the second is *contingency planning*.

Flexibility in planning

You can keep plans flexible and able to respond to changes in circumstance by building in review stages. When you finish a task, review the work done commenting on or evaluating your progress and check if the planning decisions you made for the next stage are still appropriate. If there has been a change in circumstances you can then adjust your planning.

Every time you meet a target, achieve an objective or complete a task, take a 'time-out'. Think about the work you have just completed and look at how much closer it has taken you towards your goal. Think about how you worked and try to identify how you could improve. As well as reviewing the work that you have just done, check how well prepared you are for the work that lies ahead. Ask yourself 'Is my plan still relevant or does it need to be changed?' You can work out if your plans are still relevant by asking a few more focused questions like:

- Is the goal still the same?
- Are my targets, objectives or work responsibilities still the same?
- Have any decisions been taken that affect my work?
- Are the resources I need still available?
- Are there any other changes in circumstances?

Try to keep a written record of these review stages as you check your plans and keep evidence of any changes you make to your plans. Of course changes or difficulties won't always happen at convenient times for you, for example, when you're taking a 'time-out'. They cause problems because they happen when you are not expecting them. To help you to deal with problems whenever they happen, spend time during the planning stages thinking about what things could go wrong and how you would deal with them if they did go wrong. You could go a stage further and have a contingency plan ready in the event something did go wrong.

Contingency planning

A contingency plan describes the steps you will take if something doesn't go according to plan. It attempts to address what could go wrong before it does and gives you an alternative course of action and a way to keep your work on schedule. Contingency planning is all about spotting problems that might occur and preparing for them if they do.

One useful technique is to look at your plan and ask a series of IF/THEN (or 'what if') questions. Go through your plan and assess what could go wrong and ask yourself '*If* this does go wrong, *then* what will I do?' Alternatively, you could ask 'What if XYZ goes wrong?'. Focus on important stages of your plan first, also look at the resources you need and work out what you would do if you are not able to get what you need.

You could create a two-column table and put the 'What if' questions in the left-hand column and your contingency arrangements opposite in the right-hand column. If you wanted to use the 'if/then' method instead, you could write out your plan as a series of stages and then next to each write an appropriate 'if/then' question and answer. You could also identify a suitable alternative method or piece of equipment for each of the

WHAT MAKES A GOOD PLAN?

1. Your plan should have a clear end result.
2. Your plan should be comprehensive enough to get the job done but simple enough to understand and implement. It should have a clear logic to it that others can see and follow.
3. Try to minimise risk. Have contingency plans ready to help you cope with unforeseen circumstances. Make decisions that are realistic and take account of the circumstances. This will mean that your plan is more likely to work, because it will be well thought out and feasible. Good contingency planning should cover the resources, costs and time changes needed to cope with any adjustments.
4. Be as specific and as detailed as you can when it comes to time, cost and resources.
5. Keep your plan flexible with appropriate review stages built in. By continually reviewing your plan in terms of your overall purpose and the progress you make, you will be able to adjust and adapt your work to respond to changes in circumstances. You will also keep on track!

In a group or team situation a plan should, as much as possible, incorporate the ideas of all the people who have to implement it.

resources you need to use. Things rarely go as planned, so contingency planning can be a useful way of dealing with the unexpected.

Monitoring your progress

Once you start acting on your plan you need to gauge your actual progress against your intended or planned progress. If there is a difference you need to be clear why this is the case and take appropriate action to make any necessary adjustments.

One technique that can help you to monitor your progress is to establish interim targets. These are targets that break down your main targets into smaller stages of partially complete work. The value of interim targets lies in their relationship with your timescales. They help you to monitor your progress closely and alert you to any adjustments that you may need to make. By setting yourself mini-targets you will have a greater sense of achievement and this may help to keep you motivated.

One of the main problems you will have is finding an appropriate way to record how to monitor your work. Consider using a diary or journal to keep track of your progress and perhaps produce a brief progress report when you reach an interim target. The report could be used to inform other group members, a teacher or supervisor.

See the section on **Reviewing and evaluating** to learn about assessing your planning and performance

Planning techniques to get you started

This section introduces you to some of the common techniques used to help to generate ideas and help to plan and solve problems. These techniques can be used to help you to think about your work and help you realise what might be involved in it.

There are many other techniques not covered here like cost/benefit analysis and risk assessments. These are only really appropriate in certain circumstances or are more specialised than other techniques. These techniques can also be more complicated than is necessary for a level 3 key skills course. However, you may be taking a subject (either an A-level or Vocational A-level) where they feature as part of the content; if so, you should try to use them in the key skill as well.

If you do intend to use one of the more complex techniques, identify it as a target or objective in your planning and spend time learning about how to use the technique appropriately. Identify the people with appropriate expertise or the resources you will need to help you and build them into you planning and target-setting process. Then you will be able to review how successful you were in learning about and using the technique. This could also be used as evidence of your achievements.

This section looks at:

- Brainstorming
- Spider diagrams
- Flowcharts
- Mapping

Brainstorming

This is a useful technique that tries to use creative thinking to generate as many ideas as possible about how to do something or how to solve a problem.

When brainstorming in a group you need to help create a non-threatening environment where people feel their opinion and ideas will be welcomed and valued. If people feel inhibited and don't want to contribute, perhaps because they feel they will be ignored or, even worse, made fun of, then they will not contribute. This means you will not be using the group to its full potential and the best ideas or most appropriate solutions may go unmentioned. Think of how you would like your contribution to be received and ensure that this is how you receive the contribution of others. During brainstorming sessions there should be no criticism of ideas. You must not dwell on any one idea too long. The point is to get as many ideas down as possible. You can go back and analyse the results and shortlist the best ideas afterwards.

Brainstorming is a great way to come up with different ideas about how to solve problems, start action plans or to think about contingency plans. Establish a few ground rules to ensure that the discussion goes well and appoint someone to record the ideas.

Begin by making sure that everyone is focused on the main idea or aim that you need to discuss. Try to record all ideas that are offered. Using a board, overhead projector (OHP) or flipchart is a useful way to record ideas because you may find that, by seeing ideas, other ideas will follow. You may find that having a group leader is a useful way of getting everyone started on the right lines. Leaders should define the problem and go over the ground rules for everyone. Organise your group seating to get the most from the discussion: you want to get everyone involved and interacting with each other. A circle is a good group layout; however, if someone is taking notes for the group using a flipchart or OHP then a horse-shoe shape is better.

Keeping the proof

You need to find some way of recording the brainstorming session that lets you use it in your portfolio of evidence. You should keep you own notes and thoughts on the session anyway, but work out how to make a copy of the group effort. Make sure that the person recording the notes for the group isn't tempted to start editing out ideas. You need a record of the whole event. Other things to consider include asking the people taking the notes (especially if they are not group members) to write up the notes or enter the ideas on computer and copy the information to everyone. Include the time and date of the discussion and how long it went on for. You may also find it helpful for an outsider to sit in and feed back their thoughts on the session to help you to work on improving the process in future.

Another common form of proof is a witness statement from someone who watched the group in action. You might even want to consider recording the group using a video or audio cassette. However, make sure this isn't going to inhibit people. Have the video set up at the back of the room on a stand; don't be tempted to have someone wander round with a camera. The audio cassette can be a useful and discrete way of recording the occasion and can be a helpful and cheap way to ensure that everything is recorded.

Leading a brainstorming session

There are a few simple *do's and don'ts* to follow if you are to ensure that a brainstorming session is successful. As leader you will be the person responsible for keeping the environment friendly and supportive. The rules are given in the table of do's and don'ts below.

Recording a brainstorming session

If you are chosen to record a brainstorming session, you need to follow a few simple rules. Firstly, don't edit or be selective and record only some ideas. Record them all. This will make sure that nothing is missed and people will see that their contributions are all equally valued and are

Do	Don't
Define the problem to be solved for the group	Don't allow too much time to be spent on one contribution or idea
Encourage an open, friendly, enthusiastic and uncritical attitude among group members	Don't abuse your position by speaking too much
Encourage everyone to participate	Don't allow the person recording the session to edit and choose their favourite ideas
Help people finding it difficult to make a contribution by creating an opening for them	Don't let people spend too long making one contribution
Keep everyone focused on the subject	Don't let the session drag on if everyone has dried up
Have a fixed time limit for the session to help focus minds	
Ensure that records of all contributions are being taken	

being noted. Secondly, ask people to repeat points if you are not sure what was said or if they were speaking too fast. Finally, try to do a little preparation work beforehand by finding out how best to record the contributions. If you are taking notes, prepare some paper with a column for the contributor's name and one for their contribution, or have a prepared list so that you record each idea numerically as they are made. If you are using a flipchart remember to use a dark-coloured pen, write on one side of the paper only, number your pages and try to keep each person's complete contribution on the same page. Make sure you know the names of everyone taking part.

Evaluating a brainstorming session

There are two types of evaluation worth doing if your are using brainstorming as a technique to generate ideas related to key skill work. The first is an evaluation of the results themselves.

You need to sort out the suggestions made and identify some way of assessing them to see which are the best or the most feasible. This means looking at the constraints you have (for example, time, resources, quality) and working out which ideas or suggestions are the best and are likely to bring success. To do this you could get a blank sheet of paper and draw a line down the middle, top to bottom. On one side put a positive (+) or the word 'FOR', on the other side put a negative (−) or the word 'AGAINST'. Then go on to list the advantages and disadvantages of each idea or suggestion made during the brainstorming session. Rank them using numbers if you want.

The second type of evaluation involves the brainstorming session itself. Spend a little time looking at how the session went and assess what went well, what went less well and try to think why this was the case. Look at the different factors that make a brainstorming session successful and measure how well your session went against these factors. This way you know how to improve in future.

Spider diagrams

When thinking about problems or plans people can get bogged down in detail very quickly and then begin to lose sight of the overall goal. A spider diagram can be a useful way of sketching out the main features of a problem or issue before you get too heavily involved in one particular aspect of it. It can be a quick way of getting the key features down on paper as they come to you and is a useful written record of your initial thoughts on a subject. A spider diagram can be drawn in this way:

- **Step one:** Turn your paper side on (landscape)
- **Step two:** Write the main issue or problem in the centre of the page (the body of the spider)
- **Step three:** Think about what is involved in your central issue. Then link each idea you have to your central issue by a line (the legs of the spider)
- **Step four:** Each idea can be broken down into smaller issues or themes also attached by lines. (It begins to look less like a spider at this point)

Redrawing the diagram, grouping related themes, and using colour to show connected associated ideas can help you to get a better picture of what is involved.

Spider diagrams can be used to begin to link ideas with action. For example, once you have identified all the key points relating to the central idea or problem (step 2), use step 3 to establish what activities need to take place to make each point happen. Having identified all the related tasks go back over the diagram and prioritise it by numbering the sequence to help you to develop an order for your plans.

Spider diagrams are normally drawn freehand. This allows you to sketch out your thoughts quickly without having to interrupt your flow too much.

Flowcharts

A flowchart is a useful graphic way to help you and others figure out and understand the sequence of steps involved in your work and the key decision points and consequences. A flowchart consists of a series of different standard boxes and symbols, connected by flow lines that show the major stages and decisions involved in carrying out a task or solving a problem. You should begin to construct your flowchart early on and keep adding to it and changing it until you have an accurate picture of the

Example of a spider diagram

actual stages involved. When you have a completed flowchart that accurately shows the steps involved in your work and how they work, this can be used to show others.

Constructing a flowchart can be a useful way to get a clearer picture of what will be involved in a task. It can be a useful way of uncovering hidden or unexpected difficulties and can prepare you for what lies ahead. The diagram in the margin opposite shows the main flowchart symbols, and their definitions are given in the table. However, there are many more symbols used in flowchart work than those shown here. If you think this might be a useful way to help you plan, find out about the other symbols you could use to help you draw more sophisticated flowcharts. This will help you to produce more detailed flowcharts.

Keep the flowchart logical, clear and simple, as shown in the diagram opposite. To begin drawing flowcharts, get to know the symbols and their meaning, find yourself an appropriate starting point and an aim or target as an appropriate end to the process. Then, beginning at the start of the process ask yourself what needs to be done first and what happens next. Work your way through each logical next step putting in any decision points and the consequences if the decision goes one way or the other.

At first, stick to the major steps in the process and major decisions. You can then go back over the flowchart and add further layers of detail. You can create separate flowcharts that break down large processes further to show the detail of exactly what is involved in a particular key stage.

You can attempt to have one master flowchart that attempts to document the whole process from start to finish for your work, but use it only if you feel comfortable working with it and you are confident it is an accurate reflection of what is involved. Otherwise, break the general flowchart down further into smaller, more detailed stages and treat these like smaller

Shape	Meaning	Explanation
Rectangle	Process step	This symbol is used to represent a single action, stage or step in the flowchart
Diamond	Decision point or question	These can contain 'Yes/No' options or other types of decisions that need to be made
Oval	Starter or terminator	Used at the beginning and end of a flowchart with the word 'start' or 'end' inside
Arrow	Flow line	These are used to indicate the direction of the flow
Circle	Go to	Used when flowcharts get too big for the page and need to be continued on another one. It can also be used when your flowchart gets complicated and you want to avoid arrows crossing over each other or to 'go to' a sub-routine. If you use it for this then you need an exit point (e.g. Go to A) and then an entry point (e.g. a circle indicating where you should re-enter the flowchart with A written inside it)

stages in the overall plan. It is perhaps better to create smaller flowcharts for interim targets or objectives and work with these. If you want to include a more detailed set of steps as a sub-routine then use the 'Go to' symbol as a reference in the general flowchart.

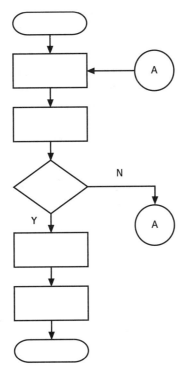

Example of a flowchart

Decision points

Decision taking using the 'diamond' symbol is straightforward. Normally when there are two or even three options they are shown leading off corners of the diamond as in the diagram below.

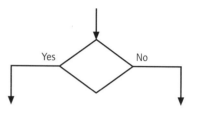

Simple two-option decision

However, if you have a number of options (i.e. more than three) then you can use the method shown above.

HINT

Many word-processing packages have draw functions that contain flowchart symbols ready to use and make up into a flowchart. Check the support literature that comes with the software you have access to and establish what the potential is to create flowcharts.

Drawing flowcharts

There are a few simple rules to follow in order to produce clear and effective flowcharts:

1. Draw flowcharts on white, plain paper using one side only
2. Use a template to draw the symbols in your final version
3. Print the contents of each box to make them easier to read
4. If you have sub-routines use the 'Go to' symbol and put them on a separate sheet of paper
5. The flow is from top to bottom of the paper
6. Arrowheads indicate the direction of the flow

Produce a simplified plan using a flowchart that shows only the main tasks and decision points. More detailed flowcharts can be used for specific targets. The simplified chart may be useful to share with others, while the

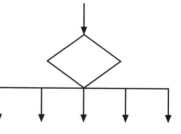

Multiple-option decision

more detailed work can be used to monitor progress. The process of drawing the detailed charts will also ensure that you confront what lies ahead and will help you to realise what will be involved.

Mapping out ideas

Mapping out ideas on paper is a useful way to develop them a stage further. It's a little like brainstorming on paper although you try to organise your thoughts in a more structured way. Mapping does this by getting you to start thinking about the relationships between different ideas. Although the process of creating a map is similar to creating spider diagram, it is a more thorough and comprehensive attempt to explore your original aim, goal or idea. You are also trying to recognise how different aspects of the work might be connected or interlinked.

Start by taking a blank sheet of paper then write your idea or aim in the middle of the page. Then write any related ideas or concepts as branches radiating from your central idea. These will be smaller tasks or related ideas that make up or relate to the main one. Each time you get a new idea start another branch and follow it through until you have exhausted the thoughts you have on it. Branch off any related points you have to consider. Try not to interrupt your flow too much by stopping and thinking about one point for too long. Concentrate on getting it all down on paper first. Try not to edit. Once you put something down, look at it to see what it will involve, and try to unpack it a little further.

Mapping will take practice to do well. It is worth trying and even your first attempts will be useful as a record of your early thoughts for your assessor, and they can also act as a reminder in case you forget something.

Some advantages of mapping as an exercise include:

- The discipline of doing the mapping helps you to clearly define your main idea
- It allows you to see all your thoughts and ideas on one page
- You can always come back to review your map so it makes recall and reviewing easier
- It makes figuring out the links between key ideas easier and lets you begin to see the relationships between ideas
- It can help you spot, at an early stage, any problems like contradictions, conflicts or gaps in your work

Once you have a map you can begin to see complex relationships between ideas and judge the relative importance of each. This can be a useful starting point for planning your work and target setting.

Techniques to use when you map

There are a few simple techniques that can be used to help you get started and to organise your work. The table below explains some of these techniques.

Mind mapping is a technique devised by Tony Buzan. Check out his great website at www.mind-map.com. You can also try a Web search using "mind mapping" as your search phrase

Technique	Explanation
Branches	An idea may lead to other closely related ideas and these can be shown branching off the idea they relate to
Arrows	Used to show links and dependency relationships between ideas
Clusters	Related ideas or branches can be grouped together when you create a second draft
Lists	Some branches may lead to a list of thoughts or factors that you want to note now but come back to later
Colour	Using the same colour for related ideas or for differentiating between priorities can be useful. Again this might be a useful second draft process to go through

HINT

Once you have a map you are happy with containing all the key points (even points that may be unlikely to be acted on), copy it. Use this copy as evidence for your portfolio. To make it a more effective piece of evidence, annotate it using a different colour of pen to help explain the thought processes that took place as you created the map. This will be a very useful way to show your early thought development and planning process.

Most people try to go from the initial mapping straight into planning. However, you should take time to look at your map once you have exhausted all your initial thoughts and try to organise them a little before you finish with this stage. By reorganising your initial map as a second draft it will become easier to follow and may make drawing up the plan a little more straightforward.

In your second draft, group related ideas together to give your thoughts a little more order and structure. Do this by drawing circles around related ideas or tasks, or by highlighting them with the same colour pen when you look over your first draft. Then recreate your map. You may want to take this opportunity to think about what you put down and to edit out ideas that may no longer seem relevant. Keep your original map to refer to just in case there is something that you dismissed but may need to come back to. It is also an important piece of planning evidence for your portfolio.

The second draft will make a better starting point for drawing up plans and it is at this stage that you should begin to introduce a time frame. Take sections of the map and try to set some timelines. There may be different activities that need to be done simultaneously so you need to start thinking about how you need to co-ordinate your efforts and how you can keep track of your progress.

Reviewing and evaluating

When you 'work with others' you are expected to review the activities and report on how your methods of working and working relationships could be improved. 'Improving own learning and performance' has a section on reviewing your achievements and progress, and 'Problem solving' will involve reviewing the approaches you take to solving problems. This section will look at ways you can review and evaluate work whether you are working in a group, working individually or problem solving.

One common fault people often make is to leave evaluation until the end, once the work is done. Evaluation should be a dynamic and ongoing process. It should take place as a natural part of the way you work.

Your own reflection

There are a number of popular sayings, usually delivered with a sigh of regret, which mean things look clearer or more obvious after the event. When you reflect back on something you need to try to resist the temptation to feel regret. Rather, use the experience as a positive factor. Reflection is the process of contemplating how things have gone. It involves some mature and honest deliberation about your own performance. It is a process designed to try to get you to learn from the lessons of the past and take your experiences and build on them.

Look at what went well and what went badly, analysing why things happened the way they did. The aim is to learn from your mistakes and build on your success. You really need to challenge yourself and ask how you could have done things differently to become more effective or successful.

The ability to reflect on your own progress and performance will become increasingly important if you continue your studies at a higher level. At college or university you will be expected to take far more control over and responsibility for your own learning and performance so taking time to develop this ability while doing the key skill will be of benefit later. The same is also true at work; self-evaluation is a sign of willingness to improve and is valued by employers.

Reflection will help you find out a little more about yourself as a learner. To do this you need to ask yourself:

- How do I work best?
- When do I work best?
- What motivates me?

Popular sayings
- 'Hindsight gives you "20/20" vision'
- 'Wise after the event'
- 'If I knew then what I know now'

Words that relate to reflection
- Deliberation
- Contemplation
- Consideration
- Pondering
- Rumination
- Personal observation

Hindsight: the ability to understand, after something has happened, what should have been done

- What has been an obstacle or barrier to me in learning?
- What has been a positive influence on my learning?
- What areas need to be developed?
- What can I attribute any success or failure to?

These become key areas to address as you learn or work on different tasks and in different situations. Gradually you will build up a picture of the type of learner you are and you will begin to see patterns emerging for success or failure. The idea is not to get too bogged down or to dwell on this but to get into the habit of spending a little time reflecting on the *hows* and *whys* that relate to your performance. Feedback can also be useful in helping you reflect on your performance.

There are a few simple things you can do to make reviewing your work a little easier to do. The first thing is to keep a journal or a diary. Write in it regularly. You will find that just by writing down your thoughts they become a little clearer and you begin to see things differently. Don't just use the diary or journal for your key skills thoughts, open it wider and also use it for any other work or courses you are doing. Regardless of how diverse the different courses and work are, you are the common factor and the journal is about your development and progress. You will find that you begin to learn from all your experiences and will be able to transfer this learning and experience to different contexts.

Another way to help you reflect on your learning and performance is to increase the amount of useful outside information available to you about your work and progress. The thoughts and observations of others you trust or respect will be a useful source of feedback. People who know your work or are familiar with your situation can offer invaluable insights and can be good objective sources of information. Even people who don't know you particularly well may have a level of insight, experience or expertise that you could find useful. This input can be added to your own thoughts and help you establish how best to improve or proceed.

Be careful not to be too harsh on yourself. Even if you get some negative feedback that may be harsh or blunt, try to look for messages or information that you can use and then move on. As you begin to reflect on the quality and appropriateness of the feedback you also get a better idea of how you can most usefully give feedback to others.

Words like criterion: standard, touchstone, benchmark, measure, and yardstick.
Singular: criterion
Plural: criteria

Why having criteria is important

A criterion is a standard on which a judgement or decision can be made. You can write them as simple statements that will attest to your ability to do something. You will be able to prove either by demonstration or through evidence you have collected that you have met the criterion. This is also how the key skills assessment works. Each key skill sets the assessment targets (these are the criteria) and you need to produce evidence to prove you can achieve them (this is what your portfolio of evidence is for). So if you need to see examples of criteria, look at the key skill specifications.

When you set targets for yourself or you try to find a solution to a problem, it is always useful to consider how you can be sure you have achieved what you set out to do. That way you are aware of the standard you need to aim for and have an idea how to prove you met it. Take your goal, various objectives or targets and think about how you could show each of these has been met. You will be beginning to establish criteria to measure your performance and success. The next issue is to make sure that others agree that these criteria do in fact show that you have achieved what you wanted to. Criteria can be written like targets but with one crucial difference, that they are about trying to measure if you have or haven't done something. You may need to consider issues like:

- What would be sufficient proof that I have achieved my objectives?, i.e. how many times might I have to do something?, or
- How can I prove I have done something successfully?

Setting criteria for success and then applying them as part of your evaluation to see how well you performed can be extremely useful. Setting criteria means that you are trying to quantify or measure your performance. After you set some evaluation criteria to help you measure your success or the extent to which you solve a problem, you should discuss them with your teacher, assessor or supervisor. You need to find out if they think your criteria are appropriate measures of your progress. If you set the criteria early enough, you can return to them as you monitor your progress and check to see if they are still suitable, and you can change or refine them as necessary.

Feedback

Feedback can be a chance to give or receive important information about how you are doing. This will help you determine how you can improve your performance based on someone else's insight and opinion. You will get a chance to help others develop and improve by offering them feedback and in turn you will be able to benefit from their perspective and opinions on your work.

People may see this as an opportunity to settle scores or to get their own back by being unnecessarily negative. There is very little anyone can do with negative feedback. It stirs up resentment and introduces bad feeling that can unsettle and damage team relationships. Try to be fair and honest when giving feedback. Treat others as you would like to be treated yourself. The watchword for giving feedback is 'constructive'. You must always try to limit your feedback to either positive remarks or constructive comments that help others understand their work or behaviour better.

Giving feedback

Keep the following factors in mind when giving feedback:

- Be honest but tactful. Try not to be blunt, emphasise the positives in others' work and be sensitive to their feelings if you are discussing performance that you think could be improved. Respecting someone's

REVIEWING AND EVALUATING | **25**

feelings, while being honest and sincere is an example of giving appropriate feedback
- Try to be specific rather than vague or general. Try to make sure that they actually get the message and can relate what you are saying to actual events or work
- Avoid the temptation to speak for others. Let people know how you feel but don't get involved in rumour or gossip. Keep it work-related and give feedback on how you thought things went from your point of view. Avoid the 'I thought you were great but I know such and such thought you were terrible' syndrome
- Don't be embarrassed about giving praise, thanks or showing appreciation when it is deserved. Explain why you feel this way and how their work or attitude was a positive influence on your own

Remember, once you are clear about the kind of feedback you want to receive then should also be clear about the type of feedback to give to others. The key words to aim for are:

- Constructive
- Honest
- Tactful
- Objective
- Appropriate
- Useful
- Friendly
- Encouraging
- Supportive

Consider how best to give the feedback. The person may appreciate a paper copy of your comments because it may be useful as evidence. Look for opportunities to use the feedback you give as evidence for your own portfolio. Your 'feeding back' on someone else's work might be useful as evidence in 'Working with others' or 'Problem solving'.

Getting feedback

The biggest problem people have when getting feedback is that unless it is praise or extremely positive, they take it negatively. There is a certain standard and quality of information and communication style you are trying to reach when you give feedback to others and you may find that though you are working hard at trying to meet these standards, you are not getting the same consideration in return. This can be frustrating. One way to try to change this type of situation is to give some feedback on the feedback.

Explain why you thought the feedback you received wasn't as helpful as you had hoped and ask if it would be possible for some further comments. You can also explain what type of information you need to get as feedback in future, explaining why this may be of more use to you. However, don't use this as an excuse to 'have a go' at the person giving you the feedback or use it as a way to even the score if you feel you were unfairly treated. Use the opportunity as a chance to explain the type of information you would find helpful. Practise your own skills by being tactful, honest and calm and share with the person why good and appropriate feedback is important to you.

How to use feedback

There are a few simple steps that you can take to help you make effective use of any feedback you receive:

1. Check that you understand what the feedback means and try to understand why you received it, i.e. what made the person make each comment in particular
2. Don't be afraid to ask follow-up questions on the feedback to help you clarify something
3. Identify the important issues that mean significant changes
4. Identify the minor issues that mean slight adjustments or just mean taking more care or time

Asking follow-up questions on feedback you are given can be a good way to get the most out of the people around you. This can be useful if these people have skills, expertise or experience relevant to your work.

LOOK ON THE BRIGHT SIDE

You will find that many people have a tendency to focus on the negatives like what went wrong and whose fault it was. In times of crisis or failure people focus more on 'blame-storming' than trying to sort problems out.

Try to be positive and help others to be positive by focusing on the problems or issues at hand rather than on individuals. Try to provide positive comments alongside any suggestions for improvements.

Helping others to comment on your work

Make it easy for people to comment on your work by producing it on computer. Set the line spacing to double or 1.5 spacing and leave large margins left and right. (This makes it easier for others to write in comments in your work at appropriate points.) Use a simple, straightforward text that is easy to read like Times New Roman or Arial and use a font size that is easy to read, for example, font size 12. Make sure you have page numbers and always include a title.

Make sure that the person commenting knows you are expecting feedback and let them know when you need it by. Remember to be polite and give them advance warning and plenty of time to comment. If you need to remind them, send them a friendly note to jog their memory.

Font styles:
Times New Roman
Arial
Courier
Tahoma

Group work

At the heart of group work or teamwork is the commitment shared by those involved. You should experience a number of benefits when working with other people. By looking at the benefits you get an idea of what you should expect from others and what others will expect from you. The main benefits include:

- The ability to share ideas
- The chance to gain different points of view
- The opportunity to benefit from other people's experiences or abilities
- Help and encouragement to keep focused and get the job done

You will also get the opportunity to learn to deal with criticism, develop the ability to give constructive criticism and gain the skills needed to deal with conflict and disagreement. These skills and abilities are all vital and will be of benefit in a variety of different circumstances.

PLANNING

Planning is a key part of the process of working with others successfully. Make sure you read through the section on planning that starts on page 5 for help and guidance on how to create a team plan and set appropriate objectives.

Dealing with people

People act and react in many varied ways. Sometimes people have a tendency to adopt ways of behaving that are more self-protective than open and co-operative. People also tend to forge alliances with friends that can frustrate others and may detract from the group and its purpose. Two things to keep in mind are who to work with and how to try to keep everyone focused on the task. The best way to deal with these issues is at an individual level by making sure you strive to be open and co-operative, and at a group level by discussing how to create an open and co-operative atmosphere.

Even when you are working with others, you need to keep in mind that it is *your own individual portfolio* that will determine whether you achieve the key skill. So even if the group is not as effective as it could be and some work or targets are being missed, you need to show that you can work with others, even if some of the others are not able to work with you or within a group. This means showing that you have acquired the necessary skills and have evidence of them in action. Such evidence will show that you can be open and are able to communicate and work effectively with others.

There are two main factors that will show a group's success: the tasks done (the ability of the group to meet its aims and objectives and how the group's performance is measured), and relationships (the ability of members to show they can work with others). Your group needs to discuss the arrangements and expectations for both.

Group leaders v. self-managing groups

When you form a group to carry out a certain task you may want to consider whether the group needs a leader or whether you will all manage the group. Deciding which organisational method is most appropriate really depends on what you want to achieve. Larger groups facing a diverse challenge tend to work best with a leader who, if nothing else, acts as a focal point. Smaller groups with a clear focus work well as self-directed groups. In self-managing groups there are no formal leaders and group members work co-operatively to organise and carry out the work.

If you decide that a leader would be beneficial for your group then you need to remember that there is a difference between leader and boss. The 'Working with others' key skill credits people who demonstrate that they can work together. This requires leaders to be more like facilitators who help the decision-making process to happen at meetings and not someone who dominates the group and gives orders to others.

It doesn't have to be as clear cut as having or not having leaders. Establish what functions need to be handled by individuals (e.g. a chairperson for arranged meetings) and consider rotating these roles around the group so that everyone gets a chance to be involved.

You will need to discuss five key areas when you begin working with others in teams. These are:

- Organisation and ground rules
- Establishing objectives
- Agreeing working arrangements
- Monitoring progress
- Evaluating the work

Organisation and ground rules

Although it may feel a little awkward, you should spend time discussing rules or guidelines for the type of behaviour the group wants to encourage. This spells out for everyone, right at the beginning, the type of behaviour expected. You need to establish early on how decisions will be made, how you will work and how problems or differences will be resolved.

When you discuss the topic of decision making you need to consider whether or not you will take decisions by:

- Majority voting
- Consensus
- Compromise, or even by

- Delegating responsibility for decision taking to one or more individuals directly involved in that particular work

Perhaps the best approach is to be flexible and to keep your options open. Particular decisions may be more important than others and your group may decide to chose a method of decision taking that is appropriate for each type of issue that arises. If this is the case then set out a few examples of the decision taking that will be used for different issues. For example:

- Seeking consensus could be used for strategic changes that affect the whole group; for example, setting and changing aims and objectives
- Delegated decision taking will be used for small-scale everyday events that may have limited consequences
- Subgroup in charge of a specific area of work will have responsibility for decisions in their area

However you choose to take decisions, make sure that there is some way of reporting them that keeps the whole group informed of events. This will also help to ensure that smaller groups or individuals don't get carried away and exceed their authority.

See the section on **brainstorming**, **spider diagrams** and **mapping** to find out how to generate ideas (page 14)

Your aim should be to make sure all members feel that they are an integral part of the team and that no one feels left out. If you notice someone who seems to be excluded from a conversation or discussion, try to involve him or her by asking that person to comment. Not only is there a team responsibility to involve everyone, there is also an individual responsibility on everyone to play their part and to ensure they do their best to help others participate. Remember there are two ways to do this:

- By conducting yourself in a way that encourages others to participate
- By actively helping others to participate

Establishing objectives

Teams need to identify and agree what their aim is. You need to establish why the team exists and what purpose it is to serve. This helps to make sure right at the beginning of the process that everyone is clear about why they need to work together and will also help to clarify specific tasks that need to be carried out. Hopefully people will feel greater commitment to the group effort if they are clear about why the group exists.

When members participate in setting the group aims, they become more committed to ensuring the aims are achieved. The aim should be to instil within the group that each person is an integral part of the team and has an important role to play in ensuring its success. The best way to do this is to make everyone feel a part of the group from the outset when you first meet, begin to take decisions and identify objectives.

The group will need to break down their aim into objectives and the related work to be carried out. A key part of objective setting is ensuring that objectives can be measured in some specific way. You will need to be able to determine whether you met your objectives and judge how well you did. Try to establish performance standards for your work and how progress can be measured. This way not only will people know what the group must do but they will also know the standards expected of them. As well as establishing how to measure your group objectives, you also need to begin to establish a time frame for all this work and begin to discuss the resources you will need.

When you establish your own role within the group you should turn this into a set of objectives with criteria to measure your performance. You need to make sure these tie into the overall group targets and on completion will have helped the group reach its collective aim. Also identify review points where you can assess your progress and consider when you need to share information or update other people, when you will need information from other people and when you may need the group to help you to make decisions.

Your individual work must relate to and involve the group. Don't be tempted to get your work allocation, then go off on your own and come back when you have completed everything. This is not working co-operatively. Make sure you identify timelines for your individual efforts that are compatible with those of the overall group.

See also: **target setting** on page 7

Agreeing on the working arrangements

You will need to spend time discussing how the team should be organised. Decide whether or not there will be a leader, or whether the group can work without one. Effective teams are made of committed individuals working together towards a common aim with each playing an important part in ensuring the team's success. So your group will need to address how it will be organised and how the work will be shared among the group members.

Establish how the group will make decisions and report progress. This may mean deciding about how and when the group needs to come together and meet. You need to arrange a programme of meetings, establish how long you think they should last and decide how participants will be notified.

Groups can communicate through meetings. This may involve one or two members co-operating on a specific project or a larger group discussing ways of sharing important information, taking key decisions and monitoring progress. Effective meetings take time, commitment and planning, and without these ingredients they can often be a waste of time.

Learn more about **holding meetings** on page 34

Monitoring progress

How is your group going to keep each other up-to-date on progress? Who needs to know what? Consider how the group will communicate with each other and share information. Businesses use memos and email; how do you intend to do it? Though sending memos or email may be seen as a chore, remember that it is not just a useful way of keeping others informed but also represents useful forms of evidence of your involvement in the work.

The key is to communicate effectively regardless of how you choose to do it, so discuss it with the team. If you are sending memos or email, discuss what should be sent and who should receive copies. It can be useful to appoint someone as an information person who gets copies of everything to keep in a central file that any one can access. This helps create an open atmosphere and serves as an information base for the whole group.

The Learning Curve

Create an effective group environment

See also: **Creating a good atmosphere** on page 46

You need to build a group atmosphere that encourages people to participate – one that is both receptive and welcoming. This helps generate enthusiasm in the group members. You can do this by setting appropriate standards of behaviour for yourself then trying to encourage them in others. You need to try to avoid creating hostile environments where participants would be reluctant to speak or to contribute ideas. This would demotivate people and problems will start to emerge as communication breaks down.

As an individual group member try to:

- Co-operate rather than compete
- Involve everyone in decision making
- Share your information and update people on your progress
- Be open and receptive in group discussions
- Make sure you are not the one intimidating or inhibiting others

Hopefully by playing your part in helping to establish and maintain the type of environment conducive to effective group work others will be encouraged to follow your example.

Maintaining good working relationships

The main ways to maintain good working relationships are to be open, receptive to the contributions of others, supportive, friendly and communicative. You need to make sure you do your best to help others to perform their tasks and meet their objectives successfully. Share information about your work and progress. Aim to find out how best to communicate with others, when to communicate and what to communicate. Find the balance that leads to appropriate levels of communication, don't swamp others with unnecessary information or keep them in the dark, guessing what you are up to.

Resolving conflict or arguments

Conflict can lead to the breakdown of working relationships and thus detract the group from its purpose. Often, given time and space, people can think about a difficult situation and return to it with a more positive and constructive attitude. So sometimes a break and a little space can benefit all concerned.

Resolving conflict is not easy but by considering a few points and acting appropriately you might be able to rebuild a positive working relationship:

- Keep in mind why the group has been formed
- Try to think and act rationally
- Avoid the temptation to take sides if matters become heated
- Keep talking, listening and stay open and approachable

Remember that any initial response you make to a comment or situation will set the tone for the following conversation so try to avoid an over-reaction or a confrontational response. Keep your side of any exchanges open, receptive, genuine and respectful. You can be assertive without being aggressive. Try to be patient with others and try to understand what could be upsetting others.

Generally, conflict is a result of disagreement about work or personality clashes. Work differences become the responsibility of the whole group to try to resolve. The group could mediate between the two disagreeing parties and try to reach a satisfactory solution for everyone concerned. This could be done with a group leader, an individual in the group that both parties trust and respect, or with an appropriate outsider. The point is to resolve differences for the good of the group in a way that both parties can agree to.

The other way to resolve conflict is to use the group to arbitrate either at a meeting or in a less formal surrounding. In arbitration both parties present their positions or points of view and the group decides. The responsibility is on the group to give both a fair hearing and to make objective decisions. Group members can take some of the potential heat or bad feelings out of the situation by finding and commenting on the good in both sides.

In this type of situation you want to try to prevent making the conflict worse. If you are involved in the conflict or are trying to resolve it, try to be sympathetic to the others' position and why they might hold it and come prepared to listen, reason and resolve the difficulty fairly. Other steps to consider include:

- Behaving responsibly and judging the argument on its merits. Try not to show favouritism
- Looking for ways to create a compromise. Identifying the common ground that might exist between the feuding parties can do this
- Ask each person what they like or don't like about the other's position

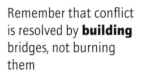

Remember that conflict is resolved by **building** bridges, not burning them

- Try to use friendly language and a soft, low tone of voice to take some of the heat out of the situation. Be objective, fair and tactful even if faced with irrational behaviour or arguments

Personality clashes are harder to deal with. This type of conflict is often best dealt with outside the group by drafting in help from an appropriate third party.

WHAT YOU COULD DO IF ONE OF THE PEOPLE IN A CLASH OF PERSONALITIES IS YOU

- Try to recognise what it is you don't like about the other person
- Try to think what the other person dislikes about you
- Try to deal with the problems without losing your temper
- Try to identify a strength or something you like or respect in the person
- Ask yourself if your behaviour is rational and justified. If not, *you* may be the problem.

If all else fails, agreeing to disagree on an issue can often be a useful strategy to resolve conflict. However, try not to bear grudges.

Holding meetings

Meetings will generally involve the dissemination of information and decision taking. They can be used to focus a group's attention on particular issues or tasks and help generate ideas to act on. They also provide an opportunity to review progress and take appropriate action if things are not going to plan. Meetings can also be a useful place for you to review and monitor the success of your plans.

You will find that by having meetings you will get the chance to show your ability to meet many of the evidence requirements for the key skill section on agreeing objectives and working arrangements in 'Working with others'.

Making the most of meetings

You may decide that 'one-off' meetings will be more appropriate than a regular meeting set at the same day and time each week, fortnight or month. Either way, make sure you will have a record of what is said and discussed. This will be useful evidence for your portfolio. Establish whether you need a chairperson to help run the meeting, decide how you will record the meetings and how this information will be distributed to the group afterwards. Rather than appointing one person to chair the meetings and someone to produce minutes, consider rotating these responsibilities around the group. This approach will provide more varied evidence for everyone's portfolio. Also discuss whether you need someone to chase progress for the group and report back. Always make sure everyone is clear about why you are having a meeting and that they know what the group needs to achieve by having the meeting. Then everyone can try to play their part in achieving it.

All meetings should have a clear agenda, given to group members well before the meeting. This gives everyone a chance to prepare appropriately. Make sure at the end of a meeting you spend a little time agreeing what needs to be discussed at the next meeting. Ensure that you discuss:

- Any issues that should be on the agenda
- Any key reporting issues that need to be addressed
- The time, date and venue of the next meeting

Try to involve everyone in meetings, this will help to make sure that everyone feels that they are part of the team.

Agendas

Be clear about the purpose of meetings and work out in advance what subjects will be discussed. You can do this by preparing an agenda for the meeting. An agenda is a formal notification of all the important details of the meeting and it is sent or handed out to those attending. It needs to contain the time, date and place of the meeting, what will be discussed at the meeting and the order topics will be discussed. This makes the meeting run more smoothly. When you come to draw up an agenda put the most important or complex issues at the beginning of the meeting. This is because people will be more attentive and focused at the start of meetings.

The outline of the agenda should be easy to determine if you have a good plan of action. Depending on the progress made, you should be able to identify items that need to be discussed. If this is not the first meeting of the team, then there will be matters to discuss from the previous meeting, updates to be made and you should have a list of items previously raised that need attention. You will also be able to refer to the overall plan of action and get some further ideas.

Normally on agendas there is a section called 'Matters arising'. As in the example overleaf, this usually appears after the agenda item for the minutes or notes of the previous meeting. 'Matters arising' covers anything that is outstanding from the previous meeting's business shown in the minutes or notes. This is the first opportunity to check on progress. You can report the follow-up work done as a result of discussions made at the previous meeting.

The agenda could also contain updates on progress in key work areas, with the person responsible for the area updating the rest of the group. You may want someone to provide an overview of progress in all aspects of the work, it really depends on what would be the best way to monitor developments in meetings.

KRUGER FRIGHT CLUB

Friday, 13 July 2000, 2 p.m.

Room 8
Basement, Jason Building, Kruger College

Agenda

1. APOLOGIES FOR ABSENCE

2. MINUTES OF LAST MEETING

3. MATTERS ARISING

4. TREASURER'S REPORT

    i. New memberships
    ii. Account balances

5. PROPOSALS FOR HALLOWEEN FUNDRAISING

    i.   Disco   Paper ref.: BOO/001
    ii. Fete   Paper ref.: BOO/002
    iii. Raffle   Paper ref.: BOO/003

6. FILM SHOWINGS

    Rod Smith to report.

7. ANY OTHER BUSINESS

8. DATE OF NEXT MEETING

Example of an agenda

Key roles in meetings

As effective members of the group, everyone has a role to play in meetings. You will be able to share information, update others and update yourself on how others are doing. There may also be decisions requiring your participation. You should certainly prepare for the meeting by reading through the agenda and previous minutes and seeing whether you are expected to contribute anything to the various items to be discussed and how you can help others to do so.

In more formal meetings it is usual to have someone chairing and someone taking notes (minutes).

The role of chairperson

A chairperson (Chair) introduces the meeting, saying a few words about the context of the meeting as well as handling any organisational issues. The Chair should be clear about the meeting's objective and the results or decisions that need to taken at the meeting. It is always a good idea to talk about this up front. The Chair needs to ensure that the agenda is directly related to the objectives of the meeting and lays out a clear path to achieving them.

They are then expected to lead the group through the agenda and control the meeting, making sure people who want to speak get a chance to, keeping the discussion on track. They are responsible for ensuring an orderly meeting that addresses all items and issues that need to be dealt with.

The Chair is usually responsible for overseeing the production of the agenda for the meeting and needs to have a clear idea of how much time they are prepared to spend on each agenda item. They also need to review any supporting material that needs to be sent out to accompany any agenda items, for example the minutes of the previous meeting, any copies of reports or presentations that will be given at the next meeting.

The Chair should sit where he or she can see each person attending so as to be able to direct the meeting. Try to end the meeting with an upbeat summary of the successes so far.

GUIDANCE FOR CHAIRING A MEETING

- Enforce rules
- Keep everyone involved
- Keep everyone informed
- Maintain a positive approach throughout

Minute taker

The group needs to decide in advance what kind of minutes should be taken at their meetings. You may want full minutes of each meeting, or perhaps a brief note outlining key issues discussed, decisions taken or contributions made will do. The example overleaf shows the general format of minutes, but the important thing to remember is that you must all be clear about what you want to achieve and the minute taker must know what is expected of them.

The minute taker normally sits beside or near the Chair. This allows them to quickly confer if they need to.

GUIDANCE FOR MINUTE TAKERS

- Don't leave it too long after the meeting to write up the minutes. Do it while it's still fresh in your mind
- Use the agenda headings as headings for the minutes
- Work out an appropriate numbering and referencing system beforehand
- Include a list of those attending
- Refer to people in your minutes by their initials

MINUTES OF THE JERSEY YOUNG ORNITHOLOGISTS CLUB
31 August 2001

Present: Ms J. Wren (chair)
Mrs L. Goosey (secretary)
Mrs C. Licken
Mrs H. Penny
Mr D. Duck
Mr B. Finch
Mr H. Martin

In attendance: Mr T. Cat

1. **APOLOGIES FOR ABSENCE**
Apologies for absence were received from Mr C. Robin.

2. **MINUTES OF LAST MEETING**
The minutes of the meeting held on 15 June 2001, previously circulated, were passed as an accurate record of events.

3. **MATTERS ARISING**
CL reported that the problem reported at the last meeting had been resolved.

4. **WINTER MIGRATIONS**
HM presented a paper (ref: JYOC/001) proposing a survey of migratory species during the month of September. After discussion, the club agree to the proposals asking that the results be reported at the next meeting.

5. **BIRD TABLE SURVEY**
TC attended for this item.

i. Survey results
TC presented the results of the survey to the group reporting that 35 people had taken part in the local area with 17 different species recorded.
ii. Continuation of the survey work
BF asked if the survey was to continue. TC replied that the plans were to continue monitoring the tables through the winter. There was a discussion on the need to include more appropriate winter food on the tables as well as a range of feeding devices. TC agreed. The club thanked TC for his hard work and asked that he continue to keep the club informed of the survey. TC agreed.

6. **RAPTOR WATCH**
DD and HP presented a paper (ref: JYOC/002) about the local raptor populations expressing concern about increased numbers. Discussion followed. Members agreed that increased numbers of top-level predators were indeed a concern and agreed to remain vigilant. The club thanked DD and HP for bringing the issue to their attention.

7. **AOB**
HM reported that he would be out of the country until May and unable to attend meetings until then. He asked that he still be sent JYOC papers. HM to liaise with LG.

There being no further business, JW thanked the members and closed the meeting at 4pm.

8. **DATE OF NEXT MEETING**
It was agreed that the next meeting would be held on 7 October 2001 at 2pm.

Example of the minutes of a meeting

ROTATION

Consider rotating the role of Chair and minute taker at each meeting. This way everyone who would like to can get a chance to experience the roles. Appoint each role for the next meeting at the end of the current meeting.

Agreeing who does what

When it comes to allocating tasks for group members you need to try to work to people's strengths and ensure you get the best out of everyone. This is more likely to guarantee success. You must try to avoid allocating tasks to people who are reluctant to do them or are not really well suited to them. When it comes to dull or boring chores, be fair and share them out evenly.

You need to ensure that everyone is clear about the working relationships and their individual and joint responsibilities. This will help avoid unnecessary duplication of effort or confusion. The minutes of the meeting can be a useful way to remind people of their responsibilities and should be circulated well in advance of the next meeting.

Playing your part at meetings

Look at your own role in meetings and see how you can work towards becoming an effective participant as an individual and team player. The first thing you can do is to be prepared. This is regardless of whether you have something on the agenda that you need to talk about or not. You may be responsible for updating people about your work; even if you don't there is still work to be done. You have a duty as a team player to ensure that the meeting is effective and the team aim is a little clearer, easier to achieve or closer to completion as a result of your presence at the meeting. This includes taking part in discussions and decisions, listening to other team members and making appropriate comments.

If you are presenting some information at a meeting try not to talk for too long and remember to let others participate. For example, don't be tempted to give some information, highlight a decision that must be taken then go on to make recommendations about what that decision should be. Stop after you have presented all the necessary facts and figures and invite others to comment. Acknowledge their suggestions, and along the way offer your own. Once you have a full range of possible solutions try to round up the agenda item by suggesting to the Chair what would be the best solution from your point of view.

In formal meetings contributions have to be made 'through the chairperson'. You need to direct your questions or contributions through the Chair to the group in general or a particular individual. This etiquette helps reinforce the formal nature of the meetings, helps the Chair control the meeting and stops people talking over each other or just shouting something out.

Before meetings, study the agenda and work out what points you would like to bring up and when to discuss them. Work out what you personally need to get from the meeting to make your team role easier to

GROUP WORK | **39**

achieve and note down where it would be appropriate to discuss this. If there is something that you need to discuss that's not covered, draw it to the Chair's attention. Many agendas have a last item that handles any other business (AOB); this might be the appropriate opportunity to discuss your issue. The Chair could mention the topic in their introductory remarks to give people prior warning that it will be discussed.

During meetings your main priorities should be to:

- Get involved without being domineering
- Be part of the co-operative effort and the consensus building
- Be receptive and attentive to the views of others
- Take notes on critical decisions or issues raised

After meetings don't wait too long before you look at your notes of the meeting. Deal with them while they are still fresh in your mind and take the appropriate follow-up action.

HOW TO BE A GOOD 'TEAM PLAYER'

- Participate in team meetings and decision taking
- Set personal targets and aims that help meet the overall group objectives
- Be sensitive and receptive to the views of other group members
- Co-operate rather than compete with your other group members. Don't sit back and watch others struggle – help out
- Learn about your other group members. Try to understand their strengths and weaknesses, their likes and dislikes. This will make working with them easier
- Resolve conflicts quickly and try not to bear a grudge
- Review your own progress in light of the wider group aims and make sure you play your part
- Try not to favour your friends' comments because they are your friends. Be objective

---

Taking part in discussions and team meetings

No doubt you already discuss different topics with friends, family or colleagues, and this section aims to help you develop these abilities, allowing you to take part in discussions regardless of who else is in the group. It will also help you to keep focused on the topic under discussion as well as show you how to help others get what they need.

SUGGESTION TO GET YOUR GROUP STARTED

Meeting 1

Meet at an early stage and have someone chair the meeting to ensure all the points are covered and that everyone gets a chance to speak. Someone should take notes on the main decisions taken and points made. Talk about the work you need to do and how best to organise yourselves to do it. Deal with the organisation, decision taking and ground rules first. Try to get down on paper:

- A description of what you will be trying to do
- Why you are doing it and what results you expect
- A rough timetable illustrating completion times of each main phase
- What you will need to complete the tasks
- Who would like to do particular tasks

If you manage to do all this you will have had a successful first meeting. If you don't manage to cover these topics, discuss how you will. Then make sure everyone in the meeting receives a copy of the notes. Consider asking the person who chaired the meeting to obtain feedback from someone appropriate, asking their advice on the suitability of the decisions taken.

By the end of this meeting everyone should be clear about the group's purpose and working arrangements.

Meeting 2

After a short period of time, when everyone has had a chance to read the notes of the meeting and has thought about how it went, meet again. Update everyone then go back over all the decisions that were taken about the group organisation and the work discussed to see if everyone is still in agreement. Try to refine the decisions a little more. Concentrate on adding more detail making everything clearer.

Everyone should be aware of the purpose and format of the meeting so they can make appropriate contributions. By the end of the meeting try to have completed a comprehensive statement that firms up the objectives, how they are to be measured, the resources needed, timelines and each team member's role in their attainment.

At this point you should be clear about your own individual responsibilities and how they relate to the team aim and the responsibilities of others.

Contributing to discussions and meetings

In an ideal discussion, everyone will want to participate and no one would say anything silly or irrelevant. All the contributions made would be useful and the discussion would be a worthwhile experience for everybody.

When you are having a discussion you may find that some people will talk far more than others, perhaps to the extent of dominating the

discussion or monopolising the meeting. Some may make irrelevant contributions or comments or wander off the topic, while others may say nothing or very little. Participants need to think about their role and behaviour in discussions. You also need to keep in mind that you will gain far more information and opinions if everyone is involved and contributing.

The first thing to keep in mind is that contributions should not be long speeches. You aren't giving a presentation; you are taking part in a group exercise. Talking for a long time, preventing others from making contributions or interrupting others are all signs that you are failing to participate effectively. The reverse is also true. Just showing up, sitting quietly and hoping that no one will notice you will also mean that you are failing to play your part.

Types of contributions

Any of the following count as making a contribution to a discussion:

- Making a point
- Expressing opinions
- Explaining something
- Asking and answering questions
- Presenting an agenda item
- Sharing some results
- Encouraging others

Concentrate on making a relevant contribution each time you speak. Don't just make one contribution then keep quiet; get involved in the discussion. When you do make a contribution show that you can adapt what you say to suit the needs of the group and the situation. For example, show that you can recognise whether the discussion is formal or informal and act accordingly or whether a point needs to be made firmly or a word of encouragement is needed. Remember that politeness is always appropriate regardless of context.

Be prepared to take brief notes during discussions or meetings. Writing down the key points made, decisions reached or who said what could be helpful when it comes to referring back to something. It is always good to correctly attribute what is said to the person who said it first. It can be a kind of compliment and shows that you are paying attention. Your notes will also become a useful record and evidence of your involvement in the discussion. The notes will also help you to check any minutes that were taken for accuracy and this helps you spot if there are any differences between your interpretation of events and other people's.

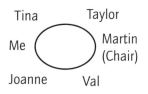

You could start your notes by jotting down the names of the people taking part, even quickly putting them into rough seating arrangements. This will help you to remember who's who. For example, look at the brief sketch in the margin; that is all it would take.

Keep your notes brief because you need to be looking at those contributing and not persistently looking at your papers. Making eye contact with others when they talk is encouraging for them.

Always
- Be aware of your surroundings and the people in your group when you make your contributions
- Be polite
- Speak clearly
- Wait for others to finish making their points
- Try to be supportive

Never
- Shout or raise your voice
- Be rude
- Get angry
- Dominate the discussion or fail to participate

Active listening

The point of a discussion or meeting is to exchange information and ideas with others. This involves giving and receiving information. The simplest way to show someone that you are listening is to look at him or her, and to jot down any key points you think are important.

There is a difference between *listening* to and *hearing* someone. You can be looking at someone and not really listening to what they are saying. You hear the sound of them talking but you're not really paying attention. People can usually tell because your eyes have glazed over, and such signs can be really off-putting. They may even notice your attempts to fight off a yawn, especially one of those 'closed mouth' yawns. To the rest of the group and to anyone watching (like the teacher assessing you) this is just like your saying 'I'm only interested when I'm talking' and reflects badly on you.

Make sure you are actually listening to what is being said. The word that typifies a good listener is *attentive*. Use different listening techniques to let others know you are taking an interest in what is being said. There is a range of verbal and non-verbal techniques that convey to others that you are paying attention and you will be surprised how important these are to the people talking to you. Just imagine how you would feel if no one looked at you when you talked. In fact, not looking at someone can be a sign of disapproval.

Attentive: to be alert, careful, regardful or observant

Look at the table below for common examples of these techniques.

Techniques for active listening

Facial expressions	These can give the person talking important clues as to how their contribution is being received. For example, looking puzzled can encourage them to explain or elaborate more about a point they are making
Body movements	Nodding in agreement can be encouraging, as can shaking your head if it matches what the speaker is saying
	Having your arms crossed could be taken as a sign of being defensive, while a slightly tilted head can show that you are listening. Maintaining eye contact shows the speaker they have your attention

Verbal encouragement or reassurance	The occasional word or noise of approval can be a useful way of offering support to someone speaking. Verifying the message by repeating it back to the speaker is a useful technique. It not only shows you were listening but allows you to check your understanding. This involves using phrases like: 'So, what you're saying then is …' 'Let me get this straight, are you saying …?' 'Am I right in thinking …?' *Affirmative verbal sounds* are the noises or words you use to show that you either agree or understand what is being said. These are useful ways of supporting or encouraging others during their contributions
Probing for further information	You can ask a speaker to go into more detail about what is being said by focusing on one point they have made and asking for more information or by asking them to expand on something. For example, consider using the following phrases: 'Is there anything else we need to know about …?' 'What do you feel is the most important …?' 'What led you to this conclusion?'

Affirmative verbal sounds: these are the sounds of agreement or understanding that you make in conversation, for example 'uh-huh', 'mmm', 'OK'

EXPERIMENT TO SHOW THE IMPORTANCE OF VERBAL ENCOURAGEMENT

Try this exercise to see how important verbal encouragement or reassurance can be to those talking. When someone chatty calls on the telephone and starts to tell you something at length, make sure you keep quiet and say nothing, make no noise at all. Not even a grunt or a 'yeh!', nothing at all. See what kind of reaction you get from the person on the other end of the phone. They will probably find it disconcerting and will keep checking that you are there and are following what is being said. This is because you are not giving any clues to show you are listening and taking in what is being said. The point is that even when you are not talking, sometimes people still need to hear the odd indication of reassurance.

When you are not under the spotlight and are in a normal conversation or discussion with family or friends, you are probably already an accomplished user of these types of gestures anyway. What you might need to develop (practise) is the ability to maintain them without being inhibited when you do your key skills assessment.

Making sure you understand what has been said
Test your understanding by rephrasing statements and repeating them to

the person who made them. It should then be clear that you have understood what was said (and that you were listening). If you haven't understood they will correct you and clarify what was said.

Techniques to help you get across a complex message

You can use a number of different ways to help others understand complex messages. One of the simplest ways to do this is through repetition. Go back over what you say and explain it again but using alternative wording. The idea is that each time you explain a concept or idea, you help more of the people listening to understand it.

Other useful techniques to try include:

- Using examples the group would be familiar with to help them understand your points
- Using figures of speech or figurative language to help the group understand comparisons or connections between things. Figures of speech add interest and impact to what you say and are useful techniques to help enhance or explain points. The common figures of speech used in presentations are hyperbole, personification, metaphors and similes
- Ask yourself out loud, during the presentation, the important questions: 'What do I mean by ...?' then answer the question for the audience.

Asking questions and responding to others

Questions and answers

When you are taking part in question and answer sessions, be aware of what you don't know. This means recognising beforehand your limitations in terms of knowledge in certain areas or topics. When you are asked something you don't know the answer to, you should do one or more of the following:

- Admit that you don't know
- Say how you could find out the answer
- Ask if anyone else knows the answer

HANDY HINTS

- Refer to the questioner's name in you answer
- Repeat the question before you give the answer. This is an especially useful tip to remember for larger groups. It allows you to make sure everyone has heard the questions and it also 'buys' you a little time to think of your answer
- Never try to make others (questioner or person answering) feel silly or awkward, even if their question or answer is irrelevant or confused. Try to be positive and helpful

---

Helping others participate

Creating a good atmosphere

One of the best ways to encourage others to participate is to help ensure the atmosphere suits discussions. This means making sure that people don't feel intimidated or worried about participating. Others will feel this way if the atmosphere is threatening and they think that they are likely to be ridiculed, made to feel silly, likely to be confronted, faced with aggressive behaviour or with being ignored. Play your part in helping to ensure that the atmosphere is light, friendly, receptive and non-threatening and show that you are *receptive* to other people's ideas, comments and suggestions.

Receptive: willing to listen to new ideas or suggestions

Sensitivity

Try to be aware of how others might be feeling when you participate in discussions. The key word that typifies the quality to strive for is *empathy*.

Empathise by imagining yourself in the other person's position, trying to understand what they are thinking and how they might be feeling about how the discussion is going. You could try to help them feel more comfortable or confident by using some of the different techniques mentioned already.

Empathy: the ability to be aware of, and understand, how others are feeling

How you behave and the tone of your voice can affect how others will react or participate. When the topic is serious, don't be *flippant*. Be positive, supportive, and friendly and choose an appropriate tone of voice that will help create a good atmosphere and encourage others to feel confident and able to take part.

Flippant: treating serious things lightly, being cheeky or disrespectful

Encouraging others to take part

Show you are able to help others to take part in the discussion. If someone is finding it difficult to make a contribution because they can't seem to get the group's attention, invite them to make their point. Create an opening for them by inviting them to speak. However, don't turn the spotlight on someone who won't be comfortable with this attention.

You can ask 'follow-up' type questions to help get someone more involved in the group discussion by asking them to *elaborate* on or explain some of the comments they have made. Ask them in a supportive way, showing that you are interested. This would be a good way to get others more involved, as long as you are sure that the person would want to make further contributions. Don't add to another person's stress or worries by getting them to be involved if they don't want to be. This is where empathy comes in. Try to judge if the person would be comfortable making further contributions. If you think they wouldn't, then don't press them on the matter.

Elaborate: the ability to expand on something said by explaining further about it or going into more detail

Using language that doesn't offend or exclude anyone

When you discuss something or present a topic you need to be careful not to *alienate* certain people in the group. You need to be aware that your gender (male or female) can influence the way you think and speak.

When you make an effort to explain concepts or ideas, you need to make sure that you do not use examples that are familiar only to you. Try to avoid using examples aimed at a particular gender. Replace these examples and phrases with more 'neutral' ones. This will show that you are aware of the potential danger of alienating those listening to you and that you are trying to involve everyone and are trying not to offend anyone.

The risk of being culturally specific is similar. Basically, it means that you have failed to take into account the potentially multi-cultural nature of your group or those listening to you and are using terms that may mean something to your own cultural group but mean nothing to others. Again, the danger here is in leaving out or even offending others.

The answer is to review your work to make sure you have been sensitive to the situation by trying to make sure what you say is understood by all.

Firm but fair

Being assertive does not mean being stubborn or aggressive. It involves being clear, concise and firm in what you say, do, or want to see happen, showing you are confident in what you say. Try to get your point of view across resolutely without being overbearing. If others can follow your reasoning, and appreciate the fairness of your line of argument then they are more likely to respect your opinion.

Dealing with dissent

When you are involved in discussions or meetings you will find that people will disagree with your opinions. People will offer alternative viewpoints to your own but you should remember this is a sign of a healthy, discursive environment. You need to learn how to handle disagreements without having them build up into arguments that become a major problem for the group.

Try to look at alternative suggestions or disagreement positively and objectively, and identify the value of what is being said. Also look objectively at your own views. The temptation is to become defensive and to stand your ground. You need to consider what others think and review your own thoughts in light of other people's reactions. Remember you are trying to show you can participate effectively in groups, not that you can win arguments. You must learn to accept and acknowledge differences of opinion and be able to reach agreement or consensus when there is disagreement.

Sexism or racism

There is no quicker way to alienate part or all of your group than by using sexist or racist language or by making sexist or racist assumptions. This is a sign that you have failed to take into account the potential nature or feelings of the people you are talking to or are making irrational and discriminatory judgements about people.

Make sure that prejudice and discrimination do not feature in your own behaviour, and don't encourage or tolerate it in others. Play a part in

Alienate: in this sense it means to make someone feel that they are not a part of what is going on and are deliberately not included

GROUP WORK | **47**

making it clear this type of behaviour is unacceptable and has no place in your group work or discussions. A lot of discrimination occurs unintentionally and is caused by thoughtlessness or flippant comments. Try to assess how best to deal with the situation depending on the circumstances. Drawing attention to a remark may make matters worse and perhaps further embarrass or upset others. Your attitude, body language and behaviour can be used to signal clear disapproval, if this is appropriate.

As a rule, racist or sexist language or comments and any other type of language that deliberately offends people are not acceptable in any type of conversation and have no place in work with others.

Try, wherever possible, to use gender-neutral words and avoid stereotypes. The most common oversight is the use of the *masculine* terms to mean men and women, for example using 'man' or 'mankind' instead of 'people' or 'humankind'.

Check beforehand, whether your remarks could cause offence. Ask yourself if they could offend someone on the basis of:

- Gender
- Age
- Race
- Disability

You are basically making sure you are not going to say anything that will alienate or offend someone or will be inappropriate. This is something you also need to remember if you are using humour or telling a joke, which should never be made at someone else's expense.

You have a right to work without feeling harassment, discrimination or intimidation. If you feel any of these three pressures, you must bring it to the attention of an appropriate person in a position of responsibility who can support you and help you take the correct steps to deal with the problem. Schools, colleges and the workplace are places that have rules, regulations and guidelines that can help you deal with these types of unpleasant behaviour. You need to find out who is best to talk to and can offer advice, e.g. schools and colleges will have a guidance or counselling team.

Non-verbal communication

Non-verbal communication is the term used to describe the messages your eye contact, body movement, gestures and your appearance send to others. These are important factors because they can be responsible for helping others to form first impressions or can help make your discussions and meetings (or your everyday conversations) run more smoothly. Non-verbal communication and body language can help you make others feel more comfortable, it can show that you value the contributions others make and that you are paying attention to their comments.

Facial expressions
Your face can reflect a lot about what your thoughts and feelings are and

you should try to use this to help convey or reinforce the points you make. The face is a useful way to 'animate' speech, bringing it to life. You know and use these everyday expressions to animate your conversation; try to make sure you also work them into your communication style:

- **Smiling**: to lighten the atmosphere and make it friendlier
- **Frowning**: to show puzzlement, disapproval and concern
- **Raising eyebrows**: to show surprise

Think of the other ways your face can convey messages or underline the meaning of what you say.

Gestures and gesticulation

You can use gestures to add emphasis to your message, for example think of the different hand gestures you use and the different contexts you use them in. The skill is knowing how to fit gestures to the time, place and subject matter and how to make them feel natural. Using appropriate gestures will help you reinforce messages and add emphasis, making your presentation more effective and more dynamic and more captivating for the group.

Common non-verbal gestures and their meaning include:

- Nodding your head to show interest and attentiveness
- Having your palms outfacing to show openness
- Tapping your foot to show impatience
- Rubbing your neck or scratching your head to show uncertainty

Hands

Hands can offer another way of adding emphasis to what you say, bringing your conversation to life. However, don't get carried away so that your hands become a distraction. Take time to look at how others use their hands to 'talk' and judge for yourself what you think is effective. Try to keep your hands free and ready to make appropriate gestures. When hands are not being used to help send positive messages to a group, you might be using them subconsciously to send negative messages.

The following will distract your group's attention, send negative non-verbal messages about you or hinder your own ability to make gestures:

- Hands in pockets (preventing you from using them to gesture)
- Hands in pockets rattling change or keys (distracting for the group)
- Fiddling with jewellery (especially rings), clothing, spectacles or a pen can be seen as a sign of stress, nervousness or even disinterest
- Doodling on paper can be a visual sign of disinterest or boredom

Eye contact

This is something you should practise. Try to involve others as you talk by making them feel a part of the discussion. You can do this by making eye contact. Try to move your focus around the group and not rest on the same one or two people all the time. Don't flit around the room from person to person. Try to focus on someone for about a sentence before

The Learning Curve

LONGMAN KEY SKILLS · LEVEL 3 · W·O·LP·PS·W

GROUP WORK | 49

moving to the next person and in this way try to include people from all parts of the group in your eye contact.

Making eye contact with different people in the group suggests to them that what you are saying is aimed at them directly. Try to avoid just gazing off into the distance or looking over the heads of the audience as if you have seen some divine light. Keep the audience alert by making eye contact with them. This will take practice and time to develop but of all the body language this is probably the most effective.

Try to make sure your eye contact conveys feeling. Eye contact is also important because it is your first clue as to how your ideas are being received.

Body language, gestures and facial expressions are a natural supplement to oral communication. You will use them in everyday conversation with friends, colleagues, parents or teachers. What you need to try to do is overcome any lack of confidence or shyness that might prevent you from using them during your presentation.

The signals that are given to show that people are attentive are:

- Nodding the head
- Eye contact
- Verbal cues or affirmative verbal noises

Reading body language

Sometimes people use body language differently. Generally speaking, women are thought to nod to show they understand, whereas men tend to nod to show they agree: the same response but two different meanings. Body language and how you use it gives you an opportunity to send positive signals to the group and helps to contribute to effective and open group or team atmosphere. However, you can also help reinforce a negative environment by using inappropriate or hostile body language.

To understand people's behaviour and to begin to try to work with it you need to be open and receptive to all the possible ways they communicate. This means:

- Listening carefully
  Firstly consider the type of listener you are: do you interrupt all the time, or cut people off so you can talk, do your eyes glaze over as you drift to a different place in your mind? If so, then you need to work on developing a better listening technique to help encourage others and to be more receptive to the contributions of others. Ensuring that you are a keen listener will also help you make sure you are less likely to misunderstand what has been agreed or to make mistakes because you haven't been paying attention. If you find it hard to concentrate or you are prone to distractions, try to focus on determining what the key points or words are, repeating them in your mind to reinforce them. Work on your non-verbal communication to show that you are both open and receptive to the person talking.

- **Interpreting correctly**

  This is when you really need to speak either to ask for further clarification or to repeat a point to make sure you have understood. Mentally repeat what the person says to check you understand it. Also look at how it is being said to get a fuller picture. Check out the speaker's body language, are they speaking with conviction? Are they being evasive?

- **Show interest**

  Leaning forward when seated can indicate interest, agreement and willingness to participate. Leaning back may convey a lack of interest. Swinging or rocking in your chair means you would rather be somewhere else or are uninterested.

- **Reduce insecurity**

  Showing that you value what others say or contribute can do this. Welcoming input from others and reinforcing their contributions with praise or thanks can also do this, where appropriate. Play your part in making the group a safe, encouraging and positive environment in which to participate and make contributions. The tone and type of contribution you make is also important, as is the body language you use and the approach you take when you are not contributing.

'WORKING WITH OTHERS' POWER WORDS

- Patience
- Empathy
- Tolerance
- Consideration
- Supportive
- Open
- Communicative
- Considerate
- Diligent

Problem solving

Making decisions

The decision-making process in problem solving is very like the decision-making process you will use when working with others. This will mean keeping an open mind, being receptive and aware of the opinions and information that surround you. There are many dangers in thinking there is only one possible answer to a problem or only one right way to proceed.

Try to be:
Receptive, aware, open
Try not to be:
Stubborn, closed-minded

Consider all sides of a problem, explore all your options and try to form a complete picture of the situation. The more information you have or are able to gather, the more effective your decisions will be. When dealing with others, consider all sides of an argument and weigh up each on its merits. That way you will be able to have an informed opinion or draw appropriate conclusions.

You must learn to separate out a range of factors that could influence your decisions or cloud your judgement. This will help you think more clearly and reason more effectively. Emotions can often get in the way of sound judgement and can influence people's ability to reason effectively. However, feelings can be important, how many times have your 'instincts' or 'gut reaction' been proved right. You should never underestimate your feelings but also try to learn to realise the effect they may be having on your decision process.

When it comes to decision making, another real pressure can be the need to act quickly. Very often, quick decisions are more about your emotions or snap judgements than about carefully considered or reasoned, rational thought. Think of the phrases used to describe decisions taken quickly:

- 'Knee-jerk reaction'
- 'Heat of the moment'
- 'Act first, think later'
- 'Snap decisions'

None of these sounds particularly positive.

You should try to take and use time effectively in decision making. This will allow you to sort out your thoughts, consider the thoughts of others, and consider all the facts or arguments and form a clear picture. Then you can act, knowing the likely consequences of your actions.

Of course, very often you must have to take a quick decision. By developing your reasoning skills you will be able to operate under this type of pressure more effectively.

What's your problem?

You need to clearly identify the main issue and then break it down into its various component parts. By breaking it down the problem may look less formidable and intimidating and therefore easier to solve. However, first you must be clear about what the problem is. By being clear in your own mind what the problem is you can avoid being distracted by minor or secondary issues. You can keep focused on what is really the issue. Too many distractions can mean that you lose sight of the key problem and become overwhelmed. You need to prioritise and focus on what is really the issue, this way you can go on to find an appropriate and effective solution.

By breaking the problem down into smaller parts, you may find that it is not as complicated as you first thought. However, you may find that is more complex. Either way, you begin to get a clearer idea of what it will take to solve the problem. Whether it is simpler or more complicated, by breaking it down you make it more manageable. This allows you to take one step at a time.

Breaking down the problem helps you to discover the scope and extent of the problem and you can then prioritise. It will also help you focus. Let's look at each of these areas in turn.

- **Scope and extent**
  Breaking down the problem gives you a better idea of the different factors involved and as a result you can begin to appreciate the resources you may need and the time it will take. It also begins to provide you with the correct type of information to allow you to start planning how to tackle the problem.
- **Prioritising**
  Once you have broken down the problem a little you can start to address which parts need to be tackled first. You are able to start ranking the different issues involved in the problem in order of their importance.
- **Dealing with distractions**
  You are looking to determine the relevant information related to the problem and need to try to sift out the irrelevant. You must consider why information should be acted on or dismissed and you will need to have clear and appropriate criteria to help you decide what is and isn't relevant.

How will you know if you have solved your problem?

You need to find a way of showing how well you have dealt with the problem or how effective your solution is. This means thinking about the actions, evidence or information that can be interpreted as proof you have found a successful solution. You must look to establish standards that will

help you show you have been successful, you have achieved your aim and the solution you implemented has been effective. These standards will also be useful in terms of keeping you focused on your targets and they will provide you with a useful way of judging your progress.

You need to determine what would be suitable targets or standards. Think about what it is you are trying to achieve as the end result and consider whether this can be broken down into standards or targets. The easiest way to do this is to imagine what a completely successful solution would look like or achieve. This should help you establish some standards or targets. Keep your standards realistic and achievable. You may be able to ask others for their opinions on what would be suitable standards to assess the solution against.

See also **Criteria** on page 24

www.qca.org.uk
www.sqa.org.uk

SET YOUR OWN STANDARDS

There are a vast number of vocational and occupational standards around that cover everything from plumbing, customer service and engineering to business management and office skills. These are normally held by organisations like the Qualifications and Curriculum Authority (QCA), the Scottish Qualifications Authority (SQA) and by individual National Training Organisations. SQA has a useful database, accessible by the Internet, that allows you to access units that contain lists of evidence requirements and performance standards in a large range of subjects. It doesn't matter that these come from Scottish courses or units because you are only looking for some ideas to help you out. Browse the websites and search for appropriate units or standards that might provide some guidance to help you set your own standards.

You should always check your final targets with your teacher or key skills supervisor.

Techniques to get you started in problem solving

There are some techniques you can use to help generate ideas, help plan and solve problems. The techniques can be used to help get you thinking about your work and what might be involved in it. The techniques looked at here are:

- Skills audit
- SWOT analysis
- Decision trees

Make sure you also look at the sections about brainstorming (page 14), spider diagrams (page 17), flowcharts (page 17) and mapping (page 21). These techniques could also be useful in exploring problems, the consequences involved in choosing different options and in helping you plan to find a solution.

Skills audit

A skills audit is a self-evaluation, it doesn't need to involve the views of other people. It is a useful way to identify the strengths you bring to a challenge and also helps you realise potential weaknesses. Though it sounds a little negative to spend time identifying weaknesses, by coming to terms with any areas that need to be strengthened you become more comfortable and confident about dealing with them or discussing them with others. You can turn the identification of weakness into a plan of action to build these up and develop necessary skills.

Start by looking at what you do well or have done successfully. Then think of the skills or aptitude needed to do this work. You are starting to identify strengths. Don't just focus on academic achievements. Then begin to narrow these down a little, looking at the strengths that are appropriate to the challenges that you face.

Consider repeating the process, looking at areas of weakness, and then see if any of these will be needed for your challenge.

SWOT analysis

SWOT analysis is a way to identify your own strengths and weaknesses and to examine the opportunities and threats you face in a more thorough and comprehensive way. It is a way of analysing what you do and don't bring to a problem or situation and the chances and challenges that await you.

S Strengths
W Weaknesses
O Opportunities
T Threats

This is a useful technique to use to help you appraise a situation. It can be a useful way to quickly identify where you stand in relation to a problem and can help you begin to realise what might be waiting for you in the form of further challenges and opportunities.

It can also be a helpful way to work out how well prepared you are and where you may need support. To carry out a SWOT analysis you need to be honest about yourself and the knowledge and skills you possess and be realistic about the challenge that confronts you. The two risks that could upset the process are overconfidence, or alternatively, being too modest. It also helps to have done a little research about the problem you want to solve or the project you intend to carry out. This way you can be more fully aware of what you are up against and this will help you conduct a better SWOT analysis. This means it might be best to do a SWOT analysis after you have explored what could be involved in a problem or project. You could also use a SWOT analysis to work out which of a number of options might be the best for you to choose.

Carry out a SWOT analysis by asking questions like those shown in the

table. Try to be as objective as possible when you answer these types of questions. To help you do this, think not only of how you might answer the questions but also of how someone else who knows you might answer them.

Strengths	Weaknesses	Opportunities	Threats
What suitable skills do you have?	Are there any skills you don't possess that will be needed?	Is there any training available?	Is there anything working against you, preventing you from being successful?
What do you do well?	What do you do badly?	Is guidance and support available?	Do you have conflicting work demands?
What useful contacts do you have?		Are there people around that have dealt with similar issues?	
What have you got working in your favour?			

Other questions like 'How much do you know about the situation?', 'How much time do you have?', 'What resources are at your disposal?' could have answers that turn out to be a strength, weakness, opportunity or threat.

Decision trees

Decision trees are tools that help you make decisions. They help look at possible alternative decisions and the implications of opting for them. A decision tree can create an accurate, balanced picture of the risks and rewards that await you when you select one option over another.

Note that decision trees can be quite complex tools to use. As a result, this section presents just a general outline of how the initial drawing process could be used to help you think through and choose between options. If you want to find out more about decision trees then make this one of your objectives as part of the key skill and seek out appropriate advice. Otherwise leave it as a way to explore the possible options available to you and as a way to think out the consequences of each.

How to draw a decision tree
Follow these simple steps:

1. Work with blank paper
2. Turn the paper side on (landscape)
3. You will be working left to right. Start the tree with a decision that

needs to be made and write this down half way down the page on the left-hand side. Use a square to represent the decision

4. Draw out lines towards the right for each possible solution you have, fan the different solutions out giving yourself plenty of space. Think of the results of opting for each particular solution. If the results are not clear then end the line with a circle, if the result is another decision then put in a square. Annotate above the circle or square with what needs to be considered

5. From circles draw out lines to show the possible range of outcomes, from squares draw out the possible solutions

6. Keep going, unpacking the different branches until you have drawn out a list of all the possible outcomes and decisions you can think of

7. Then evaluate your work

Once you have your decision tree drawn, look at each path in turn and check that you have explored and exhausted all the possibilities. Redraft the diagram if you need to. If you are able to allocate different factors like time, cost or degree of difficulty to each, this will help with your overall evaluation. If you find examples of decision trees and they look very detailed and complicated, remember that you are using them to help clarify and unpack processes for your own use. You control how detailed you need to get in order to benefit from the approach.

Rather than using squares and circles why not use exclamation marks (!) and question marks (?) instead? Alternatively, keep it very simple by putting your decision in a box at the top (centre) of a page and work down and out from there. Unpack all the different decisions, work involved and repercussions as you go. Put each resulting outcome, decision or action in its own box and then try and unpack it further as you move down the page.

For a fuller account of how to draw decision trees using this type of approach look up www.mindtools.com

There are alternative ways to draw decision trees. Find out more about them by searching the web using 'decision trees' as your search phrase

The Learning Curve

PROBLEM SOLVING | **57**

Using the World Wide Web

This chapter looks at how to find out information on the World Wide Web (the www part of web addresses). Learning how to access information held on the web will be useful because you can learn more about areas covered in the other parts of this book. The margin contains useful key words or phrases that could be used in a search engine to find relevant sites.

The web can be an important resource, helping you to find information from anywhere in the world or from just around the corner. You need to learn how to use search engines to find information efficiently and effectively. Otherwise you can waste time sifting through numerous, unhelpful websites. Learning how to make effective use of search engines and how to do searches will help you find what you want quickly and help prevent your wasting time.

The table gives you a few ideas about how the web can be used as a resource in each key skill.

The Internet is also an important link with the events and resources in your own community. People often forget that although you have access to the World Wide Web, you can also use it to search for information closer to home.

Working with others	Improving own learning and performance	Problem solving
Find out more about:	Look up reference sources like:	Find out more about techniques like:
• Non-verbal communication • Minutes or agendas	• www.britannica.com • www.howstuffworks.com • www.bbc.co.uk/education • www.gcse.com • www.learnfree.co.uk • www.mathslessons.co.uk • www.schoolsnet.com	• Mapping • SWOT analysis • Decision trees • Cost/benefit analysis
It can help you: • Gather information on companies • Investigate certain industries		

CRASH COURSE

What is the World Wide Web?
Basically, it is a huge group of files of information stored on computers around the world. Information is held in different websites and each website has its own web address (for example www.nj.com).

What is a web browser?
A web browser (or browser for short) is a software program that helps you look at files of information on the World Wide Web. It helps you access webpages. The two most common browsers are Microsoft's Internet Explorer and Netscape Navigator.

What is the Internet?
The Internet is the route webpages take to get to your computer. It is an interconnected network of computers that allows information to come from anywhere on the web to your home computer.

How does it all work?
A web browser gets hold of information through a connection to the Internet. The connection is made using a modem, a telephone line and an Internet Service Provider (ISP).

In a nutshell
Your web browser can help you get to a website using a web address and accessing it through the Internet. You access the Internet over your telephone line using a modem to send and receive data and an ISP to link you to the Internet.

Accessing the web

You will probably access the Internet via an online service like AOL or an Internet Service Provider (ISP). An online service has its own software package connecting you to the Internet, allowing you to search for information and send and receive email as well as offering a range of other facilities, e.g. news, chat rooms, buddy lists, etc., all under one roof. The illustration overleaf shows you an example of the main menu from an online service. You can see the range of different facilities including searching the web. They attempt to simplify and organise the Internet for you.

Some ISPs
BT Internet
Freeserve
Claranet
Virgin Net

Some online services
AOL
Compuserve
MSN (Microsoft Network)

BE QUICK!

Get on the Internet in the morning before the USA wakes up and logs on. Your searches might be a little quicker without all the traffic from US users slowing things up.

ISPs provide you with a connection to the Internet, making use of the software already on your computer to enable you to send and receive email through software like Microsoft's Outlook Express. You can also 'surf' on

the Internet using web browsers like Microsoft's Internet Explorer. The other common software also used by ISPs is Netscape Communicator, which combines searching and email.

You need to explore the Internet access options available to you either at home, work, school or college. Internet cafés may also be an option or a local library may provide access.

Using a browser

Most browsers work in a similar way and have a banner along the top of the screen that displays the different commands. This is sometimes called the 'standard toolbar' or 'navigation tool bar'. The main commands are described in the table opposite.

Search engines

The Internet links a vast, chaotic world of information, with no one person or company responsible for organising it. Search engines are tools to help you cut through this huge amount of information. They can quickly sift and deliver to you the information you need. They let you explore databases that contain information from millions of webpages.

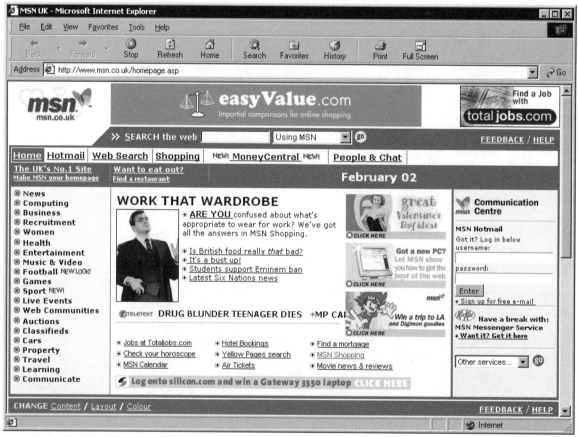

A typical web 'portal' page

Main browser commands

Icon	Effect when clicked
Address or Go to	Allows you to enter the address or name of a website
Back	Takes you to the webpage you just visited
Forward	Moves you to the webpage you just came from
Stop	Halts loading the current page
Refresh or Reload	Loads a new version of the current page, updating it with the most recent information. This is also useful if a page only partially loads the first time you access it
Home	Takes you to the page seen when your browser opens. You can customise this home page to one of your choice
Search	Begins options which search by key word
Favorites or Bookmarks	Shows you the list of websites you have entered in the past and are worth returning to
Mail	Connects to email
History	Shows you the list of websites you visited recently
Print	Prints out the webpages shown on screen

Click the Stop button if the connection is very slow and try again later

They present to you the results of your search as lists of pages that match your search request and when you decide which one is most interesting or relevant you can click on it and a link will take you straight there.

The more accomplished you become at using search engines the better quality information you will find and, most importantly, the more relevant it will be. How to access relevant information is key. Otherwise you will waste time sifting through long lists of websites that contain information that may or may not be useful. You need to develop searching skills that will help you tighten up your searches giving you smaller amounts of more appropriate information to work with.

There are several search engines that you could use and the best not only provide you with search functions but also have directories that you can browse for information on any topic.

> **HINT**
>
> Try a range of search engines and find one you are comfortable using. Then look to become more familiar with the functions and shortcuts it offers. Knowing how to use a few simple techniques that can be used in a number of different search engines will allow you to become a 'jack of all trades'. You can also become a 'master of one' by selecting a favourite search engine, learning how to use it to its full potential.

Hits: lists of matches for your search

The importance of key words or phrases in searching

The trick to any effective searching on the web is to identify the key words and phrases that will get you *hits* on sites that contain the information you need. You will be using these words to differentiate between the websites

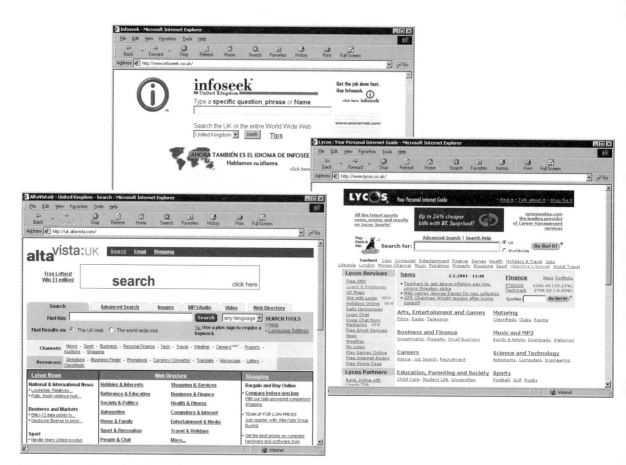

Typical search engine home pages

that you do want and the ones that you don't. This means the better the keywords or phrases you use, the more irrelevant sites you will avoid.

Regardless of what you are looking for, think of the best word or phrase that is specific to what you want to find out about. Don't choose something general, be as specific as you can. For example, if you are interested in the Manx cat (a breed of cat without a tail) don't search using 'cats' because you will get a huge number of hits about everything from the animal to the musical. Don't even use Manx because you will get lots of hits about the Isle of Man generally. Instead use the phrase 'Manx cats'. This filters out all the sites about other cats and about the Isle of Man, leaving you with results about Manx cats.

If you have received more hits than you can handle you can do a second-generation search on this list. This is called *set searching*. Search engines vary in their procedures for doing set searches, however, you normally have to enter a further search criterion like another word and select the set-searching option and the search will cut down your results further.

However, by looking at the list of hits you got in your initial search and coming up with another phrase or word to add to your first search phrases and then redoing your search, you will get the same effect as set searching.

Some search engines need you to put key phrases in **inverted commas**, e.g. "Manx cat"

Rather than look for key words or phrases in the text of webpages, you can also search in just the titles. This will mean you are more likely to get pages dedicated to your subject rather than pages where the phrase happens to appear in the text. You would enter your search phrase like this in a title search:

● Title: "Manx Cats"

Different search engines may have different procedures. This is why it is often best to learn about one particular search engine in detail, once you have found a favourite.

You can set 'Learning how to use a search engine' as one of your targets or objectives in your key skills work. As you develop the relevant skills you can keep the evidence of your improving Internet abilities by printing out the results of your searches.

Searching in plain English

By far the easiest way to search for anything on the web is to use plain English searches. Plain English searches are the best to use if you are relatively new to using the Internet. Many search engines allow you to type in what you are looking for as a simple question. They then will try to match

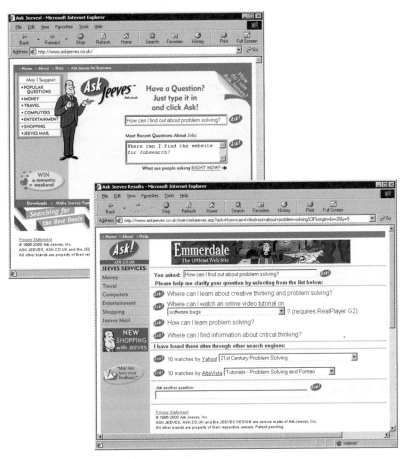

What do you need to know? Just 'Ask Jeeves' for his response!

your question to websites that may have the answer. Plain English searches can generate a lot of hits; however, the most appropriate will normally be near the top of the list.

One of the easiest plain English search engines to use is *Ask Jeeves* (Jeeves is a cartoon butler who will give you help in finding the answer). You can find it at **www.askjeeves.co.uk**. When you ask Jeeves a question he will tell you where you might find the most appropriate answer. The search engine shows you how well matched the websites are to your original question. This search engine also offers directories and reference sites to help you find the answer you are looking for.

The illustrations ask and answer the question 'Where can I find out about problem solving techniques?' as an example. Knowing what problem-solving technique you wanted to find out about in particular would mean a more accurate search.

Hint: you can print off the search results and appropriate webpages and keep these for your portfolio

The smaller illustration shows a question entered into the Ask Jeeves. Don't worry if your question is too big for the box. Just type it in and the search engine will make room in the window. For example, the full question typed in for the search shown was 'Where can I find out about problem solving techniques? The larger diagram shows the 'Jeeves' response. You can see that it does three things. Firstly it finds answers either to my question directly or to similar questions. Then it provides webpages that may have potential answers for me. Lastly, it offers me a list of websites that might be useful that can be found in other search engines.

Excite and Infoseek also provide good plain English searches.

Using advanced search techniques

There are a few simple techniques that can be used to help narrow searches down and will result in a list of hits that should be closer to your needs. The advanced search techniques involve using Boolean logic operators. The three most useful search operators involve using:

- AND
- NOT
- OR

Search engines may also have a menu of options that ask you how your keywords should be treated in the search.

- **Using AND**
  You can search for two or more key words and make sure that they all appear in the results by using AND. This will dramatically cut down the number of hits you could receive if you search without using AND. Without it you would get a far larger range of results that contains each key word on its own and in combination with the other key word. For example, if you wanted to search for information on Celtic Art and just used the key words Celtic and Art you would get a host of hits for Celtic (the people and the football team) and a massive response to the word Art. By entering Celtic AND Art your search would be reduced dramatically and the results

would be closer to what you are looking for. Remember, the other way would be to use inverted commas and type in "Celtic Art".

You can also use the plus symbol (+) instead of AND; in some search engines, for example, you would enter Celtic + Art.

- **Using NOT**
  NOT is used to exclude one word from the search. This is a way to avoid the search engine calling up hits that you know will be irrelevant. For example, if you want to learn about cooking spice, the last thing you want is a huge number of hits on Spice Girls webpages, so you would use Spice NOT Girls and save a lot of pain.

- **Using OR**
  OR searches are likely to give you more results than AND searches. This is because the command tells the search engine to show all the hits that have either word or phrase in them. However, they are useful for dealing with searches that involve topics that could be referred to in more than one way.

There are a few other common techniques like NEAR, ADJ or using parentheses to carry out complex searches combining Boolean operators. By using parentheses and combining operators you can narrow down your searches even further, saving a lot more time. If you intend to get this involved in how to use search engines more effectively, then set this as one

AND, **NOT** and **OR** are also called Boolean search operators

Examples of advanced search options (Yahoo and AltaVista)

of your targets and find out about it yourself as part of the key skill learning process.

If you look at the illustrations on the previous page showing advanced search pages on Yahoo! and AltaVista, you will see that each offers a number of ways to focus your search. AltaVista even allows you to specify where to look, e.g. the UK web or World Wide Web, what dates to cover and how to sort your results. You will find a click on link or tab that takes you to advanced searches on the main search page.

> **HINT**
>
> Most online services and web browsers have a 'Favorites' file or 'Bookmarks' where you can store your favourite website addresses. You can go straight to this file and access your favourite site directly without having to find it again or type in its address. Find out how this function works on your browser and keep useful addresses stored here. You can add to and delete addresses from your list of favourites.

The Internet addresses of some of the more common search engines are:

- Yahoo   www.yahoo.co.uk
- Ask Jeeves   www.askjeeves.co.uk
- Lycos   www.lycos.co.uk
- AltaVista   www.altavista.com
- HotBot   www.hotbot.com
- GoTo   www.goto.com
- Google   www.google.com
- Excite   www.excite.co.uk
- Infoseek   www.infoseek.co.uk

Information on the World Wide Web

Dictionaries, directories, maps and images can also be accessed on the Internet

Because there is no regulation of the content on the web, you need to be careful about the information you access there. There is no guarantee that the information is correct. You need to consider where the information has come from (is the source reliable and trustworthy?) and when it was last updated. Information from reputable organisations will be reliable but always check what you are reading.

Part 2: The Bottom Line

This part of the book shows you what you must do to gain your key skills qualification. It will show you:

- The words and ideas of the key skills
- What is expected at level 3
- What must be in your portfolio of evidence

This part starts with an introductory section **Preparing a portfolio**, and then looks at the actual evidence requirements for each of the three key skills:

- **Working with others** (WWO)
- **Improving own learning and performance** (LP)
- **Problem solving** (PS)

Each section will cover what you need to do and the knowledge, skills and understanding you need to demonstrate at level 3. The section then goes on to look at the key skill evidence requirements. Sometimes, it can be difficult working out what the key skill specification actually wants you to do so this part of the section looks at what you need to do and tries to explain the key skill requirements in plain English. In case you are still a little unsure, it explains the requirements again putting them another way.

Each section finishes with some handy hints for collecting evidence, and some suggestions about what might be in your portfolio of evidence at the end of each stage of the key skill.

Qualifications and Curriculum Authority

The key skills specifications are published by the QCA, and are widely available through schools, colleges, training establishments and awarding bodies. They are also available on the QCA website (www.qca.org.uk).

Preparing a portfolio

Who is an 'appropriate person'?

The key skill often mentions using an appropriate person, appropriate people or 'others' for support, feedback or consent. Generally speaking, anything that concerns the amount or type of evidence you collect or relates to the quality or suitability of your work, e.g. targets or plans, should be discussed with your tutor or whoever is responsible for assessing your final portfolio of evidence. Discussing these issues with the person who eventually assesses your work helps them become familiar with what you intend to submit as evidence. They can offer advice on what they would expect to see in your portfolio. Also consider people with relevant experience or expertise as useful sources of support and feedback. This could mean that other teachers, colleagues or classmates could be useful sources of assistance. Perhaps someone in the wider community may have useful skills or expertise.

As part of the early planning process for any key skill you should establish the people you need to contact and liaise with. This is absolutely essential when health and safety issues are relevant. Build in a review of possible health and safety issues at the start of your work and make sure you get the correct health and safety advice. You may also need permission to do or use certain things; again seek the appropriate advice, guidance and permission from the right people. If you are doing something career related like training and development, then a careers adviser or line manager would be appropriate. If you are intending to use equipment, you might need to discuss what could be borrowed with a technician. If in doubt, your tutor or trainer will be able to advise you on where to go.

Complex work

By asking that your work be sufficiently complex, the key skill aims to make sure you take on tasks that are challenging and appropriate for a level 3 course. If you are going to focus on using work or activities taken from your A-level, Vocational A-level, NVQ 3 or other similar level 3 course for your key skill evidence, you should expect this work to be complex enough.

Generally speaking, work will be seen as suitably complex if it needs to

For further more specific guidance relevant to each key skill see the beginning of the evidence section for the key skill you intend to do

SYNONYMS

Here are some others words that can also mean *complex* to help you get an idea of the standard of topic you are required to do:

Complicated, involved, convoluted, intricate, not straightforward.

be broken down into a series of interrelated tasks containing problems or issues that need to be separately addressed. The tasks involved, and the links between tasks, might not be clear and the situations that confront you and the resources you need may be unfamiliar to you.

What about your portfolio?

Building your portfolio of evidence

You portfolio of evidence is the work that you have done proving you can do what the key skill requires. It is the proof you will need to get final key skill certification.

A key skills unit is quite a large amount of work. It is roughly the same size as a GNVQ unit or an A-level module. So you may have to carry out a number of different tasks to have sufficient evidence to show you can meet the key skill requirements. Make sure your portfolio is well organised and that the work inside is clear and easily understood.

EVIDENCE

Evidence is the proof that you can do what is required in order to get the key skills. It is proof that you have learned about the key skill and that you can use and apply what you have learned.

The simplest approach to collecting and keeping your evidence is to have it in a separate folder or portfolio. This is by far the easiest way to organise your work and to keep a record of what has been done and what's still to do. Consider using the following handy hints as a way of organising your work:

- Have an index page that you keep updating as you build up your evidence. This should show where evidence can be found to meet each part of the key skill requirements
- Keep records of when you collected your evidence and where it came from (e.g. which A-level or Vocational A-level unit)
- Use the titles given to the different evidence requirements (e.g. 'Exploring problems and options' in 'Problem solving') to divide up your portfolio

- Copies of work are acceptable if the actual key skills evidence is part of another course
- Keep a checklist of all the things that you must cover in your portfolio (e.g. group work and one-to-one in 'Working with others')
- Annotating work to show how it was produced and how it meets specific parts of the assessment can also be helpful

Evidence matters

Examples of evidence include items you have made, material you have written, computer printouts and diagrams you have created. Artwork, photographs, audio and video recordings are also acceptable as evidence for your portfolio. Records of performance evidence can also be used. This may be in the form of testimonies from other people like a teacher, or people you have worked with, or observation records from people watching you perform the tasks. You may be able to get a statement from an employer about your ability to meet aspects of the specifications.

You need to discuss with your teacher or assessor the kind of evidence you are likely to produce and the forms this evidence might take in your portfolio. It is always a good idea to make sure the person assessing your portfolio is comfortable with the types of evidence they are likely to find in it. This also gives you the opportunity to make sure you know exactly what will be expected of you. This is especially important if you intend to submit observation records and checklists detailing your performance.

The person assessing will be interested in the following issues with regard to your evidence:

- **Validity**: does it show that you meet the key skill requirements in an appropriate way?
- **Authenticity**: is it your work?
- **Sufficiency**: is there enough evidence?

Quantity is not a measure of **quality**

If you keep these things in mind as you build your portfolio you will prevent problems arising later.

One issue that relates to group work is the separation of your work and performance from that of other people. Discuss this issue as a group and work out how you will tackle it. The records of the group decisions and your role in them could be used as evidence and it will help you and the person assessing your portfolio to gain a better idea of your own coverage of the key skill requirements.

The issues as far as you're concerned are: 'What group records do I need for my portfolio?' and 'What records of my own individual performance will I also need?'. Keep in mind that although you may be working in a group, the key skill and your portfolio of evidence are personal things. You need to prove that you have personally met the requirements and you should construct your portfolio with this in mind.

Remember that the same piece of evidence could be used for more than one key skill. For example, you may have evidence from your problem solving that will also show how you were able to work with others. In this type of situation you need to check that the evidence does actually address both key skill requirements in an appropriate way. Then you need to ensure that it appears in an appropriate place in each portfolio of evidence.

Paper trails

When you are working on the key skills you will probably find that a great deal of the thinking and decision taking can be done in your head and dealt with quickly. This won't help the person who has to look at your portfolio and decide that you have met the key skill requirements. This doesn't mean that you need to generate lots of paper-based evidence just to prove that you are doing everything required. You need to try to make sure that you have enough evidence to show how you are working without creating evidence for the sake of it.

Work you would not normally consider as evidence can count as evidence in your portfolio. Diaries and journals, sketches or ideas like mind maps, decision trees, flowcharts, notes from meetings can all be used if you remember to include clear explanations of what they show. Use the evidence you generate naturally as part of your working methods and development process for your portfolio. You should also include the various drafts you may produce.

Draft copies with annotations showing the changes that need to be made are a useful way of showing how you revise and develop ideas.

Mind the 'interpretation gap'

The secret to success in generating evidence portfolios is to close the 'gaps' that exist in different people's understanding of what the key skill specification means. The main gaps exist between what you think is required and what your teacher or assessor thinks is required. There is no point in submitting a portfolio for assessment that the teacher thinks does not adequately meets the key skill requirements. With this in mind, you need to make sure that you and your teacher have the same understanding of what the key skill is asking you to do. This may seem obvious but when you work with specifications, you may think they mean one thing while your teacher has a different interpretation. The only effective way to close this gap in understanding and interpretation is in discussion with your teacher or assessor. You are aiming to ensure that you both have the same understanding of what is expected of you and that there will be no surprises when you hand in your evidence.

You should try to build in a series of reviews with your teacher or assessor. You can use each review to go over how your portfolio is developing and keep them up to date on the types of evidence you are collecting. Ask them about whether you have sufficient evidence to show that you have met the key skill requirements. Try to take responsibility for your own evidence generation and collection and share your progress with your teacher or assessor. In this way, the key skill is a little different from

other courses where a teacher may have more control or responsibility for your work and the rate at which you do it.

You are not alone in making sure you share an understanding of what the specifications require. The other important gap exists between the teacher/assessor and the outside person from your awarding body, who will be finally assessing the work or sampling your teacher's assessment of key skills work. Your teacher will have to go through a similar process and work to close the gap between their understanding and the outside body's understanding of what is appropriate key skills assessment practice and evidence.

Here are a few examples of issues you need to discuss with your teacher or assessor and be clear about from the start:

- For 'Working with others' you need to make sure you agree with what constitutes a *substantial example of work* and what qualifies as sufficiently *complex work* with your tutor or assessor before you get started

- For 'Improving own learning and performance' make sure you establish what constitutes a *substantial example of work* and an *extended period of time* with your tutor or assessor before you get started

- For 'Problem solving' you need to make sure you agree with what constitutes a *substantial example of work* and what qualifies as a sufficiently *complex problem* with your tutor or assessor before you get started

Working with others

What the unit expects

What is level 3 all about?

At level 3 you will see that there are basically three types of evidence you need to generate. You will need to show you can:

- Plan your work
- Work towards agreed objectives
- Review your work

This particular key skill asks that you provide two types of working with other people: group work and one-to-one. Take this into account when organising your portfolio and when tracking your evidence as it builds. Though the following guidance is written as if you were working as part of a group, most of it applies to your one-to-one situation also.

It also assumes that you are involved in a group task of sufficient size and complexity to allow you to generate evidence for all three sections. This will be by far the easiest way to generate evidence and to organise your portfolio. By being involved in major group tasks from start to finish, you will find it easier to comment on your original plans and your working methods in light of your experience.

IMPORTANT MESSAGES!

You are expected to provide at least one substantial example of meeting the evidence requirements for all three parts of the WWO key skill. You are also expected to show you can work in both one-to-one and group situations.

There will probably be restrictions or conditions relating to how you should do the one-to-one and group work. Make sure you know what will be expected of you if:

- You intend to do the one-to-one and group work as part of the same activity, or
- You intend to do both separately as different activities

Be careful when choosing a partner in one-to-one work. The other person cannot assess your key skills work as well as be your work partner. So if you are going to work with your tutor or teacher someone else will have to assess your WWO key skills work.

Substantial examples of work

You are asked to provide a substantial example of meeting the standards for WWO. A substantial example of work will include a number of related tasks with some tasks dependent on the successful completion of others. Substantial examples of work are likely to take some time to complete and to reach a satisfactory conclusion.

By doing larger and more involved (substantial) work you are more likely to have sufficient opportunities to meet the level 3 WWO demands. The requirements for 'complex' and 'substantial' work are used to ensure the work you do is suitable and sufficiently challenging.

How big should a group be?

The best size of group really depends on the nature of the task that you intend to do. Too large a group and too small a group will cause problems. For example, if the group is too large:

- It will be difficult to control and organise
- Finding time when everyone can get together will be a problem, e.g. for meetings
- Communication and updating can be difficult
- Keeping everyone, involved, informed and motivated may be more difficult
- Work can be too fragmented and there is a risk of duplication
- Organising the group can be a job in itself

However, if the group is too small:

- You may find it a struggle to meet the evidence requirements
- You may miss out in developing a range of group working skills
- There can be too much work to go around
- Conflict as a result of increased pressure may arise

Think through the type of work and challenges you want to set and use this to help determine an appropriate group size. Think who would be interested in working towards the same goals, what types of skills do you need? Then make sure your teacher or assessor is happy with the size of group that you propose to work with.

What type of group work can we do?

You are able to choose work from a range of possible sources. You can use academic or vocational studies, your workplace or even a leisure or recreation pursuit, e.g. a club you belong to or a hobby you share, as a possible activity. The only requirement relates to the complexity of the work. Your teacher or assessor should be able to discuss any ideas with you and help you determine if they are suitable.

Evidence for level 3 (WWO)

Group evidence v. your own evidence

Keep thinking of what you need to have in your portfolio of evidence to help show that you actually met the key skill requirements. There will be three types of evidence that you will have to manage and discuss with other group members:

1. The evidence relating to general group work showing interaction with others
2. The evidence associated with your own individual responsibilities within the group
3. The evidence collected by other people showing their own individual responsibilities

You need to have an individual portfolio that will show that you were able to meet the evidence requirements of the 'Working with others' key skill, so though you may be involved in a group activity you must also think about your own evidence needs.

Consider asking a teacher, tutor, assessor or other appropriate person to speak to the group and offer advice about how to manage this process best. You must keep an eye on how your portfolio is developing and ensure that you have sufficient records of your taking part in group work and fulfilling your individual responsibilities within the group.

What your evidence might look like

You need to consider what form your evidence will take. Consider including in your portfolio evidence reports which describe the activities and outcomes of the planning process. Make sure you have clear statements of objectives and group members' individual responsibilities. You also need to have evidence explaining the time frames and how you will take decisions.

Records from an assessor who observed your discussions with others could be considered. Remember to clearly differentiate between your individual evidence and records and what might be held collectively as evidence for the group. At some point you will need to ensure that you have sufficient evidence of your performance to meet the key skill requirements in your portfolio.

Planning work

You will find out that having an actual written plan gives everyone something to focus on for discussions and decisions and can be a useful way of making sure everyone agrees to the group objectives and time frames. Having a plan will provide a physical record of the decisions and agreement processes that went into meeting this aspect of the key skill for the group working together. You should also work together to agree contingency plans, interim targets and begin to discuss how you can monitor and review your progress.

Making your voice heard

You must take an active part in group decision making showing that you can be an effective group member. This will mean making constructive suggestions and showing you can take into account the views of others.

Group objectives

The group needs to be clear about why it is working together and what the end results are expected to be. Then you will also be able to identify and agree clear and straightforward objectives everyone can understand. Keep your objectives realistic, measurable and feasible.

Everyone should participate and feel that they have made a contribution to the overall group objectives. This way each member will feel a sense of ownership of the group objectives and will work more effectively as a team member, feeling like they are a part of the team. Play your part and encourage others to take part.

Not all the objectives need to be related to the work. Consider some that relate to the team performance and working process. These can be objectives that feature as individual targets as well for all team members. These type of objectives could relate to:

- Maintaining co-operative relationships
- Active participation in decision taking
- Encouraging others
- Communicating effectively with others in the team

Who does what?

Three Ts
Targets
Tasks
Time

The group will need to decide what roles are needed within the group and allocate specific roles and responsibilities to individual group members. Don't just make arbitrary decisions about who carries out different aspects of the work. Try to make good use of the different group members' talents to ensure the best people for particular jobs or responsibilities are actually doing these tasks.

Roles to consider

Your group might want to consider the following roles and responsibilities:

- **Team leader**: discuss whether this role is necessary and, if so, what
  you expect of the person that assumes the role
- **Progress chaser/co-ordinator**: to help keep track of work and keep
  everyone informed of progress, making sure members are
  communicating effectively
- **Chairperson, minute taker (for meetings)**: these positions can be
  rotated from one meeting to the next as long as there is continuity in
  creating agenda items and in the decision-making process
- **Specialist positions**: are there specialist roles best organised by just
  one or two individuals, e.g. resources, health and safety?
- **Group record keeper**: remember the importance of having evidence.
  You might want to consider having someone responsible for tracking
  and keeping copies of all the paperwork and records relating to all
  group activities, creating a central file for evidence that all group
  members can have access to

Once you have allocated the tasks as a group, try to build in a little time
to allow individual members to reflect on their roles and responsibilities.
Then meet again to review, confirm or amend any decisions that have been
made. The goal is to make sure that everyone is happy about what they
have to do (their role in the team) and that they know what will be
involved and expected of them.

Working arrangements

The group must set the tasks in some sort of time frame. This means looking at deadlines for the overall work and working back, allocating time
frames to the individual tasks to help you meet your deadline.

You also need to consider how and when you communicate with the
other group members and how and when they need to communicate with
you. Keeping each other informed of progress will be vital if the group is
to meet its objectives. It is worth making group communication an item
on the agenda of your first formal meeting. Make sure the minutes are an
accurate account of the discussion and decisions taken referring to group

communication. If you are going you use meetings as a way to update and take decisions you need to consider how often you need to meet, how will the meetings be organised and how will the administration be handled. If your group is not going to have meetings how else will you keep each other informed?

Other issues to consider as a group include:

- How the group will actually take decisions
- How to respond to changes or unforeseen circumstances
- How to deal with and resolve conflict

Decision taking is an important part of any group work. You need to consider how you can involve the whole group in key decisions. This will help keep people motivated and encourage them to feel a sense of responsibility and commitment to the process. Establish the different levels of decision taking and where you are going to make them. For example, be clear about what the whole group should decide and what decisions individual members can take.

Ideally, you want to devolve some responsibility for taking decisions to individuals. This is part and parcel of having individual responsibility. By allowing individuals to take appropriate decisions, the group will stay motivated. However, you need to make sure individuals know that they need to take these decisions responsibly and are accountable for them. This means that people should know to ask others or bring something back to the whole group if they are unsure or not confident about taking a decision.

> ## DEVOLVE
>
> Devolve means passing some responsibility for decisions down and away from central control, i.e. from group leader to appropriate group members, from supervisor to the individuals being supervised.

Having some level of individual decision making also stops the group becoming too bureaucratic. It prevents the whole group from being 'bogged down' with lots of little decisions and prevents people who may be unfamiliar with the situation or the facts influencing the decision. However, there will be a level of decision taking that should involve the whole group. Generally, these will involve significant issues. Try to ensure everyone is involved and participates in this level of decision taking. Issues that should concern the whole group relate to:

- Decisions that affect whole group work
- Decisions that influence the work of others
- Changes to objectives
- Changes to timelines
- The reallocation of tasks

Each individual, once they have been allocated a role or responsibility, needs to spend time working out their own individual targets and timelines. These must be compatible with the overarching group target and timelines. Once you have drawn up your own targets and timelines, distribute them to other group members so they to can be absolutely clear about what you will be doing. This is also a good way to make sure you have fully understood your role within the group.

Resources

Resources cover:

- Equipment needed
- Time available
- Help or support available
- Money needed

Include where you will be working as one of the issues you need to consider. The group also needs to discuss any access issues to equipment or materials and must address any health and safety issues. The group must also get a second opinion or advice on health and safety from an appropriate person once a strategy or plan has been developed. It is worth singling this issue out for special attention if it is of particular concern for your work.

A 'WORKING WITH OTHERS' JOURNAL OR DIARY

- List the group targets and your own targets
- Explain how your targets relate to the group's
- Explain how your work relates to or involves the work of others
- Map out the group timescales in one colour
- Map out your own time commitments in another colour
- Record all meeting dates
- Record all relevant smaller meetings with individual group members
- Keep 'to-do lists' and reminders written in it

By the end of the planning phase everyone should:

- Feel they played a part in setting the objectives
- Contributed to deciding the working arrangements
- Be clear and comfortable with their own role and responsibilities
- Be clear about the roles and responsibilities of others
- Be familiar with the deadlines
- Be committed to the success of the group and see their success as the group's success

Collecting evidence

You need to work with the group to establish a set of realistic objectives relating to a substantial and complex task and establish what must be done to meet the objectives. Then:

- You need to decide who does what
- You need to establish roles and responsibilities based on an evaluation of what needs to be done
- You need to agree working arrangements to help carry out the tasks

Evidence requirements in a nutshell

This section of the evidence is about showing you can take part in setting up a team that has clear and feasible objectives for a carrying out a substantial, complex activity. Having agreed the objectives you need to:

1. Identify what work needs to be done to achieve them
2. What resources will be needed
3. Allocate roles and responsibilities within the group
4. Establish the working arrangements that ensure you can carry out your individual and team responsibilities effectively

HINTS FOR PLANNING WORK

- Organise your portfolio in a way that helps you ensure you have sufficient evidence to cover all the requirements, e.g. one-to-one and group work
- Keep all records of meetings (agenda, papers, minutes, your own notes, etc.)
- Get into the habit of reviewing meetings you attend in your journal or diary
- Identify early on who you can use for advice and help and when you will need their input

Working towards agreed objectives

This section of the evidence is concerned with the group in action, going about the business of achieving the agreed objectives. The evidence requirements are concerned with evidence that shows both the collective group effort and your own individual contributions. You should keep this in mind as you gather your portfolio of evidence.

This section works on two levels. If you are working in a group it concerns your work as part of this group. If you are working with one other, it relates to your own individual contribution and the dialogue and contact you have with the other person. When working with the group keep thinking about your role with others operating effectively as a group and in relation to your own individual contribution.

Your team needs to know how to realise your objectives by working effectively with others. There are three areas that your working with others efforts needs to focus on:

- Resources
- Time
- Working methods

Resources

You need to get hold of resources and make effective use of the people around you. This includes people who could be useful in terms of giving help or advice. Identify useful sources of help, advice and feedback. The people you should make use of will depend on the work you are doing. At some point it will be useful to have contact with the person assessing your portfolio, sharing your thoughts with them.

Resources can include:
Materials
Tools
Equipment
Money
People who can give advice
People who can offer support

> ## PEOPLE WHO MIGHT PROVIDE USEFUL SUPPORT OR FEEDBACK
>
> - Other group members
> - Subject teacher
> - Supervisor
> - Manager
> - Health and safety officer
> - Guidance teacher
> - Trade union representative
> - Audio-visual technicians
> - Caretaker staff (e.g. janitor)
> - School or college management
> - Local businesspeople

Who to ask for advice or feedback will depend on what you need help with. For example, a guidance teacher may help you with group dynamics and any problems you might have, while a health and safety officer can comment on what you need to consider when using equipment. You may need permission from a relevant teacher or supervisor to access equipment.

Time

You need to show that you can manage your time effectively. This means making sure that you set realistic deadlines. You need to judge how your working with others can be scheduled alongside your other commitments to ensure you meet your deadlines. This means showing you can prioritise. You also need to show that you can judge when you should share your progress with other, updating them and also recognise when you need to check on others' progress.

You will be expected to carry out your individual responsibilities to agreed timescales and to the agreed quality standards. If you need to change any of these then you need to consult the group and discuss with them the reasons why.

EVIDENCE FOR LEVEL 3 (WWO) | 81

Working methods

Your own safety and the safety of others is very important. This means making sure you know how to use and care for tools and equipment correctly and making sure you and others are aware of the relevant health and safety steps you must take. The group (and you personally) must take health and safety issues seriously seeking advice from appropriate people and following the guidelines at all times.

Establishing and maintaining co-operative working relationships

You need to show you can form and maintain co-operative working relationships with the people you need to work with or come into contact with. The key skill emphasis is on working relationships, which means knowing when and how to offer support, share resources and help others to ensure success. It also means being decisive and objective when dealing with group meetings.

To be an effective team player you need to:

- Be conscientious in carrying out your own work and responsibilities
- Be able to offer constructive comments and help
- Show a willingness to communicate and keep others informed of your progress
- Be receptive to the views of others in the groups
- Try to bring the best out of your other group members. This means playing your part in creating a positive group environment making sure that there is no tolerance of intimidation, harassment or discrimination. Make sure you do not exhibit any of these traits yourself and show no tolerance of them in others
- Create an environment where everyone pulls their weight and no one is exploited, having to take on more than others

You must set appropriate standards for yourself and not encourage or condone inappropriate behaviour in others. You can make good use of the successful working relationships you establish by asking people for peer reviews. These can serve as evidence for your portfolio.

You really need to discuss how to deal with conflict when the group first comes together. If you have to deal with hostile or unfriendly people make sure you don't do anything to escalate the situation. In a one-to-one situation you need to think about how to resolve conflict and still meet your targets.

Keeping others posted

By setting yourself interim targets you can break down your work into manageable chunks allowing you to review your progress more easily. This also gives you a chance to update others of your progress. You need to evaluate your work in terms of the timelines and quality of work expected of you. You then need to decide how best to communicate your progress with the other group members deciding who needs to know what. Ensure that there are no surprises for anyone in the group as you carry out your responsibilities. This means keeping appropriate people posted about changes to timescales, quality or the nature of your responsibilities.

You can only really judge what is an appropriate level of contact with others by knowing how your work is linked to the work of others and by understanding what they expect from you. You need to agree what should be communicated, how it should be communicated and when.

Making changes

Both at an individual and group level you need to monitor the progress of the different work and responsibilities against the planned timelines and expectations. Decisions will have been taken and plans drawn up based on expectations or circumstances that could change. You need to establish how the group will respond to change and take any necessary decisions to adapt working methods or arrangements. In working out how you deal with change in your personal responsibilities you need to make sure you consult appropriate group members.

Collecting evidence

WHAT YOU NEED TO DO

You need to show you can be effective and efficient in organising your work and in meeting your responsibilities.

When it comes to those you are working with you must set up and maintain co-operative working relationships and sort out how you will deal with any difficulties. You must also show you can keep others informed of how your work is progressing in relation to both the expected timescales and quality, discussing and agreeing any changes to your plans to help meet your objectives.

Evidence requirements in a nutshell

You've already established your objectives so you now need to focus on working efficiently and effectively, meet with the people you need to work with and share appropriate information. To do this:

1. Sort out your working priorities and act on them accordingly to meet your responsibilities
2. Show you can work co-operatively with other team members
3. Resolve any problems that arise
4. Show you can share accurate information about your progress
5. Agree changes that are necessary to ensure you achieve the objectives

Reviewing activities

This whole section is about you questioning how you did both as an individual group member with your own set of responsibilities, timescales and commitments and as a group. You need to learn to reflect on your individual and group performance and look for good ways to judge objectively how well you did.

Once you are clear how well you have done in relation to your task, the key skill gives you the opportunity to explain how you would do things differently based on what you now know.

As you review your work, always try to look at your own individual contribution and how effective that was. Think of how you performed as a team member in relation to meeting your individual responsibilities and objectives, what factors influenced your work and how you could improve as a team player.

Then also consider the team's performance as a whole. The team could hold a debriefing session to evaluate and discuss their performance. If you decide to do this make sure people know about it well in advance and have time to prepare notes and organise their thoughts.

Journals and diaries are useful ways to record your thoughts on your own personal performance and the group's performance.

Agree how successful you have been

You can do this by assessing how well you did in meeting your objectives. Reflect on your own performance in meeting your responsibilities and also record your personal observations on the group performance. Your observations on both your own performance and that of the group should be objective, rational, clearly explained and justified. You need to identify what would be appropriate criteria to judge the work of the group (and yourself) against.

Hopefully you will have considered factors like 'How will I know if I have been successful?' during your planning phase.

What factors are affecting your progress?

Consider all the stages of the work, including planning, implementing and working relationships. Look also in more detail and consider things like resources, decision making and communication. Were there circumstances beyond your control that affected how you worked? Was motivation an issue?

The factors that affect your work can be positive and negative influences. The important thing is to be honest, and where mistakes have been made acknowledge them and show how you would avoid making the same mistakes in future. Show how you have learned from your mistakes. Where there have been positive influences try to reflect on how you can improve on them further.

The table shows areas that may have gone well or badly that you can address when you reflect on your performance.

Areas to consider	Types of question
Your targets	Were the objectives realistic and easy to measure or too ambitious and hard to assess?
Resources	What influence did they have on your success?
Planning	Was your plan flexible enough to adapt to changes or was it too rigid and difficult to adapt to changes in circumstances? Were the time frames appropriate or timelines too tight? How well did your monitoring and interim reviewing go?
Changes in circumstances	Were you prepared for changes? How well did you cope?
Role of others	How useful is the feedback you are getting?

Could do better?

Consider how you could improve working relationships and your working methods based on your experiences.

Start by asking yourself:

- Should I (we) have done things differently?
- If I had to do it all again what changes would I make and why?

You have the benefit of hindsight and you need to try to show how you would learn from your mistakes. You should address questions about both your own performance and the group's performance. Consider how you made decisions, how you organised yourself as a team and how you communicated, as well as your individual performance.

Hindsight: the ability to understand, after something has happened

Collecting evidence

This is where you need to show you can reflect on how things went. This means evaluating how successful you were in terms of meeting the objectives. Explain what factors had an influence on the outcome.

You also need to spend time looking at how the activity could have been carried out differently in a way that would have enhanced the work with others. You also need to agree how you could improve how you work with others in future.

Evidence requirements in a nutshell

The overall purpose of this section is to review work with others and agree ways to improve collaborative work in future. Your review must involve:

1. An assessment of how well you met your objectives
2. Identification of factors that had an influence
3. Agreement about how you could improve

HINTS FOR REVIEWING

- Keep a log so you can note down thoughts as you go
- Spend time on your own role as well as on how the group performed
- Statements from other team members can be used as evidence of how well you performed as team member
- If asked to give feedback on other team members' performance, be fair and considerate

Improving own learning and performance

What the unit expects

What is 'Improving own learning performance' all about?

Although the key skill talks a lot about learning, it is also about setting targets; turning targets into an action plan; implementing plans and then reviewing progress and achievement. It is really about teaching you a useful methodology for improving your learning and performance.

What is level 3 all about?

There are three stages involved in improving your own learning and performance, these are:

- Agreeing targets
- Creating and using a plan
- Reviewing your progress and achievements

Basically, this is a good way to work whatever you do, so think of it as continuous process that provides a useful framework to help you organise your efforts.

The key skill can help you improve on any aspect of your life. It is trying to help you learn effectively and purposefully and have this reflected in improved performance. You can choose to focus on improving:

- Part of your academic or vocational studies
- An aspect of your training
- Something related to your job or career
- A leisure pursuit, or even
- An aspect of your personal life

You are able to identify and try to meet new demands in any aspect of your school, college, work or home life. However, before you go too far in choosing your focus for the key skill, look at the type of learning and evidence requirements that you need to show. This will give you a better understanding of what might be a feasible focus for your efforts. You can see the different learning styles that you need to show in the 'Using your plan' section of the evidence requirements.

Evidence for level 3 (LP)

Agreeing targets

What's meant by an extended period of time?

This particular part of the key skill evidence requirements asks you to agree targets and plan how these can be met over an extended period of time. By setting targets to achieve a significant and challenging goal you will automatically need an extended period of time. The more time you make available, the bigger the improvement you should aim to see. Allowing more time will mean creating more space to develop your learning, skills and performance and more opportunities to practise or test them out.

When gauging how long you should take, consider the following suggestions:

- At school or college a term can be useful as a time frame because it provides natural breaks (e.g. half-term or holiday weekends) to build in smaller targets and review stages. This would also be sufficient time to develop, practise and finally evaluate suitable improvements in your learning and performance
- In a workplace situation three months should give you enough time to set yourself meaningful goals, challenge yourself and build enough time to review your progress and make any necessary changes to your plans. Over longer periods of time, you may even tie the key skill into personal reviews with your line manager or supervisor

The above suggestions are only guidelines. Very often you will find that by choosing an appropriate focus for your key skill, a suitable length of time will also come to you.

The key skill is trying to tell you that you really need to get involved with something significant and not something small or trivial that can be done in a short period of time. You need to focus on meaningful goals that you can work towards over time and that will mean you make important personal progress. By taking time, you will have more opportunities to plan appropriately, monitor your work, try different methods or techniques out along the way, improve your chances of success and, most importantly, you will have time to generate appropriate types and amounts of evidence.

Make sure you agree with your tutor or assessor whether your targets and the time frame are suitable before going any further.

Substantial examples of work

You are asked to provide a substantial example of meeting the standards for LP. A substantial example of work will include a number of related tasks with some tasks dependent on the successful completion of others. Substantial examples of work are likely to take some time to complete and to reach a satisfactory conclusion.

By doing larger and more involved (substantial) work you are more likely to have sufficient opportunities to meet the level 3 LP demands. The requirements for 'complex' and 'substantial' work are used to ensure the work you do is suitable and sufficiently challenging.

IMPORTANT MESSAGES!

You are expected to provide at least one substantial example of meeting the evidence requirements for all three parts of the LP key skill. You are also expected to show you can work in both one-to-one and group situations.

If you are not able to meet all the evidence requirements for the different learning styles in one substantial activity, another activity can be used to address the remaining learning styles. However, you need to ensure that all sections of the LP key skill are addressed in any additional activity you do, if you want to use it as evidence for your LP portfolio. This means you need to agree targets, plan, implement your plan and review your progress and achievements for all activities used as LP evidence.

What you must learn to do

This part of the key skill is asking you to show you can create a coherent and sensible way to achieve what you want. It is easiest to think of the key skill evidence requirements as being divided into three separate stages when it comes to 'agreeing targets'. You need to have evidence of goal setting, target setting and planning.

Goal setting

Establish what you want to do and identify sources of information to help you achieve your goals. Use this information to help you work out more clearly what your goals are and how you could achieve them. Doing some early fact-finding and some investigation into the different resources you might need and whether they are available or not will pay off in helping you identify realistic and achievable goals.

Target setting

Make sure the targets are *clear*, *measurable* and *achievable*.

- Clear targets
  While it is acceptable to have your goal written as a general statement

of intent, your targets must be clear, precise and easy to understand. Targets either break down your overall goal into a series of small, incremental steps (each becoming a target) or they can 'unpack' the goal by breaking it down into smaller discrete targets. Make sure you spell things out in your targets. This way planning how to meet each target becomes easier, as does assessing whether you have achieved it or not

- **Measurable**

  At some point you are going to have to show whether you have met your targets or not. You will find that this process is easier if you have short, focused and simply written targets. When you write your targets try to make them quantifiable. This means writing them in a way that allows you to tell if you have actually met them or not or that allows you to see how much of the target has been met

- **Achievable**

  Your targets must also be realistic. This means you must try not to be too ambitious. Ensure you are able to achieve your targets given the time you have available and the resources you have at your disposal. Basically, keep the challenges you set yourself within your reach

Make sure your tutor, trainer or assessor or other appropriate person agrees that your targets are suitable.

Planning for action

You will need to show you can turn your well-thought-out targets into a plan. Start by identifying action points for each target and put them in order of priority. Add in realistic timescales and identify the support you will need in order to achieve each target and how you will get this support. Support might include special coaching, guidance from key people, special classes you need to attend or questions you need to ask.

Build in 'time-outs'. Just as some sports coaches call 'time-out' to rethink their strategy and adjust their plan, you should do the same. Build in stages where you can review your progress, reflect on what went well and what went badly and make adjustments to your plan. This reviewing process is crucial if you are to learn from mistakes and keep your work on track.

Your plan needs to be flexible, and while building in 'time-outs' will help give you opportunities to respond to unforeseen changes, you also need to think ahead and consider factors that might affect your work. You need to ensure you meet your targets successfully and early identification of factors that might affect your success makes sense. This way you can prepare strategies to help you cope with change or even exploit opportunities should they arise. The main factors to consider that could affect your work are:

- Finance
- Resources
- Health and safety
- Other people
- Other commitments

Measurable:
something you can assess, gauge, quantify, demonstrate

- Conflicting deadlines
- Changes in your own motivation

Consider everything that could possibly make conflicting demands on your time or could change. You need to think ahead and consider how you would minimise negative changes and maximise positive ones. Contingency planning can be one way of preparing for anticipated problems.

Contingency plan: a backup plan in case something goes wrong

Collecting evidence

WHAT YOU NEED TO DO

Goal setting

Carry out some research and investigative work to help you answer the following questions fully:

1. What do you want to do?
2. How are you going to do it?
3. What factors could affect your plans or success?

Target setting
Write clear and realistic targets based on the information you collected and the answers to your questions. Make sure appropriate people agree these are suitable targets.

Planning
Construct a plan to show how you will meet your targets and manage your time effectively. Include details of alternative action you could take if something goes wrong.

Evidence requirements in a nutshell

This part of the evidence is about establishing what you want to achieve, converting this into realistic targets and then producing a plan of action.

So when you have a good idea of what your goal is, you need to refine it a little. You do this by finding information that will help you work out what you need to do and what might influence your work or your progress. From this preparation work, you need to set yourself some realistic targets, agreeing them with suitable people.

Develop a plan to help you meet these targets, making sure you show how you will manage your time and how you will deal with any difficulties that could occur.

HINTS FOR AGREEING TARGETS

- Think in three clear stages: goals, targets and a plan. Then make sure you have evidence of each and how you turned your goals into targets and targets into a plan
- Techniques like brainstorming, spider diagrams and mapping can help you break down your goal into targets
- Write your targets in the active voice

Using your plan

Background information

This section is about implementing your plan; turning it into action. As you implement your plan you will also need to monitor how well it is going and make any necessary changes along the way. Take a moment or two to look at the evidence requirements for the 'Reviewing progress and achievements section'. You need to review your work on two occasions. At least one of these occasions will be during the course of your work and you should build this into your planning. The other most obvious opportunity to review your work is at the end of the process though it doesn't have to be.

When you build in a 'time-out' to review your progress and perhaps look at generating some evidence for the last part of the key skill, try to get it to coincide with meeting some interim targets or with a natural break in your work. Plan for it and work towards it.

> It can be a little tricky trying to work out exactly what is expected of you in this part of the LP key skill. There are a lot of different requirements to try to address. Discuss the evidence requirements with your teacher or supervisor and make sure you are both clear about what the key skill expects you to do.

What you must learn to do

Prioritising

You may have lots of different tasks to do so you need to work out what is done first or what is most urgent. You also need to establish whether some tasks are dependent on the completion of others. This gives you two criteria to start prioritising your work. There could be others; for example, you may not need information immediately but may need to deal with the task of getting it sooner rather than later. For example, you need to send a letter requesting information and although you don't need it right away it may take time to be sent back. Work out a list of everything you need to do and sort it in terms of what is most urgent, and what is dependent on other tasks. This will help you work out the best order to do the tasks in, then try to create a timetable to help meet your priorities. This is another layer of detail that is added to your planning. Create a table that lists your priorities and gives a time frame for each. Keeping notes explaining why you prioritised in the way you did will also be useful.

Monitoring

There are two aspects to monitoring your progress: factors affecting your progress and revising your planning. You need to show that you can deal with factors that are affecting your progress and that you can keep on target. Hopefully, you will know what might go wrong and will have identified a way of dealing with it before anything does go wrong. This goes back to spending time on putting plans together and making contingency arrangements. You need to think about having a backup plan or alternative options ensuring you stick to schedule.

You also need to keep reviewing your plan and revising it when circumstances change or as you discover better ways to work. This will show that you are able to adapt and cope with difficulties or changes and make necessary adjustments to your work.

Many of the skills involved in successfully monitoring your work are related to those involved in reviewing and evaluating your progress. Monitoring is a way of evaluating how well you are doing in relation to your plans and your final targets. This way it helps prevent you from drifting off target and keeps you focused.

Feedback

Feedback can be an important way of evaluating your work, so build in ways of getting feedback. You need to ensure feedback comes from appropriate people and that it comes in a form that you can use. Appropriate people will be able to comment from experience giving useful feedback as either advice or comment on your progress. Identify at an early stage people who will be able to help you with feedback and how you will work them into the process.

Learning approaches and styles

You need to make sure that you use appropriate learning styles and approaches for the tasks that you do. You need to show you can improve your performance by studying a complex subject, learning through a complex practical activity and can carry out further study or practical work independently.

- **Studying a complex subject:** Learning here will be directed and controlled more by other people (e.g. teachers, trainers) and would normally involve attending classes, training sessions or tutorials
- **Practical activity:** This can still be as directed as the more study-based type of learning but is more about your applying knowledge, skills and understanding through activities like problem solving, experimentation, simulation, role play, fieldwork. You get to put into practice what you have learned elsewhere or to learn by doing

Both these examples tend to take place in a controlled environment of some sort where someone else sets the pace and is responsible for creating the learning environment. For example, a teacher decides on the equipment to use, the experiment that takes place or the content that should be taught. You also need to show that you know how to learn effectively in a situation where you have a greater amount of responsibility and control over the learning environment. Independent learning through practical work or investigation or your own personal study is one way to show you can take more control over your own learning environment. For example, distance learning and open-learning packages and materials may come with some direction and control requirements

The LP key skill expects you to improve your performance by:

- Studying a complex subject
- Learning through a complex activity
- Doing further study or practical work that involves independent learning

but they are designed to be more flexible than other forms of learning, allowing you to take some of the responsibility yourself. This might be anything from what, how and where to study or even judging for yourself how well you are doing.

Independent learning is a good way to focus on something of particular interest to you without having to spend time on other things that are of less relevance. You can pursue particular areas of interest in more detail and at your own pace. When working independently, start with the basics and build from there when you begin learning something new. Don't be tempted to get hold of lots of books or other sources and start studying about the most complex things straight away. Gradually build up confidence and momentum by making sure you have grasped the basic concepts first.

KEEPING AN LP DIARY OR JOURNAL

Try to keep a diary or journal separate from the actual work and tasks and use it to comment on what you are finding out about the learning process itself. Use it to write down your thoughts on your own performance, your successes and failures. Because it is private, be honest. Write in it as you would a normal diary. Try not to use it to write drafts of targets or plans or any work related directly to working towards your targets, rather write your thoughts, fears and own personal observations about your progress.

Try to do it as you go, so you can look back at the end and remind yourself of the thoughts you had at the time. Don't be tempted to leave it for a while and go back and try to remember what you thought. One of the most important things to try to do is to keep it ongoing. To make this more feasible, get into the habit of making brief entries that summarise your thoughts. That way it will be less of a chore.

Try to write about:

- How you feel about the targets you set and how you expect them to go
- What worries you about the tasks you have set yourself
- What surprised you (good or bad)
- Comments about the usefulness of resources (not specific resources like books or webpages but more general comments about the school or college library, specific search engines and useful websites)

As you come into contact with different Internet search engines you may find some easier to use than others or some that suit you better. Keep a record of these search engines and their Internet addresses, as well as a reminder of why you thought they were useful. Keep records of useful Internet addresses.

If you don't think you are going to be conscientious enough to enter information into a diary regularly then find some other way of recording your thoughts as you go along. Perhaps you could take a copy of your evidence as you generate it and note your thoughts about it on the copy.

By learning how to use different learning styles effectively you will be able to respond to new demands and challenges.

Meeting new demands
This is really about using your own experience to deal with a new set of demands or situation.

Collecting evidence

WHAT YOU NEED TO DO

This is where you show you can organise your time and your work effectively. You need to prioritise your activities and monitor your work in relation to your plan. This will mean adapting your plan if you need to, revising it to meet changes in circumstances.

You will also need to show you can find and make use of relevant feedback and support to help you meet your targets.

As you implement your plan in an effort to meet your targets, show you can select and use ways of working and learning to meet new demands.

Evidence requirements in a nutshell

Now you have a plan, this part of the evidence is about implementing it.

You need to show you can order and organise your efforts by prioritising and managing your time in an effective way. Make any changes to your plan to make sure you complete your tasks. You need to seek out and make good use of feedback and support from relevant sources to help ensure you meet your targets.

Make use of different ways of learning to improve your performance showing you are flexible and can adapt your learning to meet new demands.

HINTS FOR PLANNING

- Make sure you have a written record of what you think might go wrong or what might affect your work
- Keep records of your contingency plans
- Keep notes on who will comment on your work, and why they are appropriate people
- Keep records of the feedback you received and what you did with it
- Keep records of how you prioritised your targets and tasks in your portfolio

Reviewing your progress and achievements

Background information

This section is about appraising your own performance and showing that you can learn from it. The aim is to keep building on your strengths and working on your weaknesses, trying to improve on them. So a key factor is honesty. The key skill isn't looking for you to try to prove that you were great at everything and met all your targets easily. It is looking for you to show that you can assess what went well and worked for you and why this was the case. You also need to show you are aware of what didn't go as well and why. You then need to show you know how to work on these weaknesses and have some ideas about how to put them right.

What you must learn to do

You will need to review your progress on two occasions and establish evidence of your achievements. The most logical way to do this is to build in an interim review stage when you have made a significant amount of progress (e.g. a half-way point) and then carry out a final review at the end. However, this doesn't have to be the way to do it. If you are looking to make ongoing improvements over a longer period of time you may choose to have reviews taking place during the actual process. During each you can take stock of how you are doing and make the changes you think are necessary.

How well are you doing?

This section and the next discuss the process of improving your own learning and performance. They are not about discussing your targets.

You need to try to give an honest appraisal of how you feel you are doing. You need to think about which learning styles work best for you and provide information about what you learned and how you have learned. You are being asked to reflect on how far you have developed as a result of your key skill experience and what you are discovering about yourself as a learner along the way. Here are some questions to help you get started:

- What have you learned so far? Do a little 'before and after' analysis and discuss the ground that you have covered in between
- Do you find target setting and planning useful techniques to help you learn more effectively?
- How well is your plan working?
- How good an independent learner are you?
- Which learning style brings the best performance out of you? Why do you think this is the case?
- How well are you taking advice and using feedback?
- What learning skills are you developing or improving?

- Is there anything you have learned while doing the key skill that you will use in future?

Each of the answers to these questions could be explained and it is always helpful to provide relevant examples of what you mean.

Reviewing your achievements during the course of your work is slightly different from reviewing at the end of the whole process. During the course of your work the reviewing process should influence and change the way you work if change is needed. The review will look at the progress you are making in relation to your plan, targets and timelines. You should also use this as an opportunity to evaluate some of the earlier decisions you made with regard to resources. Based on this information you should adapt your plans and targets if you need to.

What factors are affecting your progress?

You also need to discuss the influence of factors that affect your work. These can be positive and negative influences. The important thing is to be honest and where mistakes have been made acknowledge them and show how you would avoid making the same mistakes in future. Show how you have learned from your mistakes and are improving your techniques and your learning methodology. Where there have been positive influences try to reflect on how you can improve on them still further and how you can make the most of these successful factors in other aspects of your learning. Show that you have ideas about how to capitalise on your successes.

The table below shows areas that may have gone well or badly and what you should address when you reflect on your work. Remember to explain why you think things worked or didn't work and give examples to help illustrate your points.

You will probably find that some things are not clear cut and there will be aspects of planning that went well and aspects that went less well. Concentrate on showing you know what worked and can be built on and are also aware of what needs to be improved.

Areas to consider	Types of question
Your targets	Were the targets realistic and easy to measure or too ambitious and hard to assess?
Resources	What influence did they have on your success?
Planning	Was your plan flexible enough to adapt to changes or was it too rigid and difficult to adapt to changes in circumstances? Were the time frames appropriate or timelines too tight? How well did your monitoring and interim reviewing go?
Changes in circumstances	Were you prepared for changes? How well did you cope?
Role of others	How useful is the feedback you are getting?

Showing your achievements

In the target-setting section, the importance of identifying ways to measure your success was discussed. You need to be able to collect evidence to show your achievements.

Start by dealing with the targets you met successfully. How can you prove that you achieved these? Then focus on the targets that you did not meet and explain why these were not achieved. Did you meet these targets in part? Were there circumstances that prevented you from meeting them? Did something go wrong?

Failing to meet targets is not necessarily a bad thing nor will it count against you in collecting evidence for this key skill. As long as you can explain clearly why targets were missed, and are able to show you have learned from the experience, this is still useful evidence. Consider providing a brief account of how you might tackle things that didn't work differently based on your experience.

Evidence showing your achievements could come from tutors, work colleagues, managers or anyone else who can comment on your progress. There may also be physical proof or evidence in the form of examples of your work that show you are now performing at a more competent or higher level.

The evidence you collect must help prove that you have met your targets fully or have met some partially. When you fail to meet a target, provide an explanation of why you think you didn't meet it.

How can you improve?

This last section is about rounding the whole process off by presenting a strategy that can help you continue to improve your performance. After reflecting on how you did during the learning and improving process and reviewing the outcome of the process, i.e. the targets you did and didn't meet, you need to pull all this together and show how you can build on this and improve. How can you improve based on the whole experience?

As well as collecting your own thoughts on how to improve, ask for feedback and comment from others. Get feedback from people who are able to comment on your learning and performance and have had a chance to look at and comment on your evidence. The more familiar they are with what you have been doing, the more insightful the feedback should be. At this stage, the most appropriate person may be your tutor, teacher or assessor. Discuss with them how you can improve in relation to the specific targets and tasks connected with the key skill but also in relation to learning generally.

Collecting evidence

Meeting new demands

There will be times during the course of your work when you are faced with a new challenge or find yourself in an unexpected situation. Unforeseen circumstances or unexpected changes may also make new demands on you, or you may have missed something in your planning or target-setting process. All these examples are opportunities to use your experience, initiative or imagination to respond to the new demand effectively.

This evidence requirement also asks that you include evidence of how you have used learning from other tasks to meet new demands. It can be a little confusing to work out what the key skill expects from you here; however, any evidence you have showing that you were able to use your experience (which, after all, is learning from other tasks) could be considered.

WHAT YOU NEED TO DO

Review progress on two occasions.

Each time you need to show you can draw everything together and measure the success of your learning and performance. This means providing evidence on the quality of your learning and performance experience. You must also discuss the factors that affected the outcomes. Explain which targets were met, backing this up with suitable evidence of your achievements.

When you were confronted with a new or unexpected challenge, how did you use learning from other tasks to respond to it?

You then need to discuss your performance with appropriate people and agree how you could improve it further.

Evidence requirements in a nutshell

You need to show you have learned from your experience of target setting, planning and implementing your plan and can work out how to improve your work performance.

As part of this process you need to establish evidence of your achievements and assess the quality of your learning and performance. Make sure you discuss factors that affected the learning and performance. Show what targets you met, backing this up with appropriate evidence.

How did you respond to a new demand or an unexpected situation? Were you able to use learning from other tasks to respond to it? Share your thoughts on your performance with appropriate people and work with them to establish ways for improving further. This review process must be done twice.

HINTS FOR REVIEWING

- Be prepared to discuss your successes and failures
- Note down who helped you improve your performance and why they were appropriate people
- Consider keeping a diary or journal that you use to log progress and day-to-day developments. This might be a useful way of reminding yourself of what went on when you look back on your work

---

Problem solving

What the unit expects

This part of the book tells you what you must *do* to gain the key skills unit 'Problem solving', level 3. Other parts of the book will help you gain the knowledge, skills and understanding you need or show you where to find opportunities to generate appropriate evidence.

What is level 3 all about?

The evidence requirements for 'Problem solving' cover the following three areas:

- Exploring problems and options
- Planning and implementing options
- Checking your results and reviewing your approach

The key skill requires that you carry out a substantial activity involving working on a complex problem. The two key words are *complex* and *substantial*.

What is meant by complex?

In a complex problem the solution or how you achieve it may not always be clear or obvious and there may be difficult decisions to make or issues to resolve. A complex problem will normally contain a number of smaller problems and it will be affected by different factors. There must be several ways of tackling the problem and you may have to use a range of different methods and resources to help you find a solution. Complex problems could involve any of the following features:

- Abstract ideas
- Sensitive issues
- Difficult detail
- Unfamiliar situations
- Unknown factors or variables

The term 'complex' is used to ensure that your chosen problem is at an appropriate level of difficulty to be treated as a suitable challenge at level 3. Make sure you check that the problem you will be tackling is of a suitable degree of difficulty. You can do this by discussing with your teacher or assessor your plans and thoughts on what you might do.

What is meant by substantial?

You need to provide at least one substantial example of meeting the standard for all three parts of the evidence requirements for 'Problem solving'. This is a way of ensuring that you will have sufficient evidence in your portfolio worthy of a level 3 standard and demand and that you benefit from following the methodology that the key skill is trying to put across. This is why the word 'substantial' has been used in the key skill.

Focus on a problem large enough to allow you to follow the three sections of the key skill through from start to finish. Think of something you can really 'get your teeth into'. This will give you a chance to look at the problem in detail, find a possible solution, work towards the solution and review your end results.

As you move through the different evidence requirements keep checking with your teacher to make sure that you have sufficient evidence for each section in your portfolio.

What is a problem?

When you want to bridge the gap between your current situation (where you are now) and a desired situation (where you want to be) with no apparent way of doing it, then you have a problem. In other words, how to get to where you would prefer to be is the problem.

Here are a few examples to illustrate the range of possibilities:

- Diagnosing faults and repairing equipment
- Improving the performance of a system
- Becoming proficient in a particular software package
- Organising an event, performance or fundraiser
- Designing or making something to specification
- Findings ways to reduce waste or cost

Any learning situation where you don't understand something or any practical challenge that you might face could be seen as a problem. Note that in the examples given each problem could be broken down into more precise statements about the problem or could contain a number of smaller, subproblems.

Other words that mean substantial:
ample, big, significant, considerable, sizeable

Methodology: a particular way to do something, a structure or procedure to follow

Evidence for level 3 (PS)

Exploring problems and options

Knowing that a problem exists

You need to look at defining in a clear way exactly what the problem is. Ask yourself 'Why is this a problem?'. By assessing why something exists as a problem, you begin to get ideas about what you need to do to solve it. Try to think clearly about how this problem has come about. What caused it? If something went wrong, establish when and why you think it went wrong.

Explore the problem

This is where you need to break the problem down into smaller issues, or subproblems, if this is appropriate. Breaking it down into smaller problems also gives you a clearer idea of how to find solutions and how different events and activities might need to be sequenced in your plans. This will also help you become more familiar with the *extent* of the problem.

> **Extent:** the range or scope of something

Consider conducting a 'skills audit' or SWOT analysis to determine how prepared you are to tackle the problem and what you will need in terms of help and support. This is also a useful stage to use techniques like spider diagrams or mind maps to help you think through the extent of the problem and what might be involved. The more detail you get on the problem and the more you think about what is involved, then the more information you will have to help you plan how to tackle the problem.

Establishing criteria for assessing solutions

Having thought about the problem, you now need to think about the possible solution. You need to work out how well you have done in terms of solving the problem. This means establishing some way of assessing how well you have done. This section is encouraging you to think about how you will know if you have solved the problem or not.

> **Criteria:** standards used to make judgements about something; they are benchmarks or gauges used to measure

You need to think about how you will know the problem has been solved. You can get a better idea of criteria or assessment standards for measuring your problems by asking others involved what they expect from you, by looking at relevant sources of information or by talking to people who have dealt with similar problems.

The types of criteria you use really depend on the nature of the problem you are trying to solve. Make sure they are clear, appropriate and can be used to measure or gauge whether you have been successful or not.

You must check with your tutor, teacher or assessor that the criteria you will use are appropriate and that they are comfortable with them. Consult your teacher as you draw up your draft criteria or standards for assessing your problem. Look at their suggestions and then finalise your criteria, making sure you have taken account of their suggestions.

You are going to come back to this work when you evaluate the success of your problem solving.

Find ways to tackle the problem

Having found out all you can about the problem, attention turns to deciding the best ways to identify different options for solving the problem. You need to establish which method is best suited or most likely to generate options for tackling the problem.

Basically, the key skill specification is asking you to use appropriate methods to find ideas about how to solve your problem.

You could consider any of the following methods to establish options for solving your problem:

- Discussions or consultation with others (e.g. brainstorming sessions)
- Looking at solutions to similar problems
- Learning from other people's relevant experience
- Using your own initiative and imagination
- Simulating the problem in some way to find out more about it (e.g. role play, 3D modelling or drawing depending on the nature of the problem)

The key skill will ask for **three** possible options that could be used to tackle the problem.

Weigh up your options

Once you have a range of ways that you could use to solve the problem, decide which is the most suitable. Consider what the end result of taking each option might be: how close will each particular option get you to where you want to be? Having thought about each option in terms of the outcome it could deliver, weigh up each in terms of what might be involved in carrying it out. Think about each option in terms of the *resources*, *risks* and *rewards* it will involve.

- **Resources:** Determine what support from other people will be needed. Other resources may include time or money, e.g. for expenses if you need to buy anything or travel
- **Risks:** These include any health and safety issues that may relate to practical work, visits or any other aspect of what you propose to do.

This part is worth discussing with other people to make sure that all the necessary precautions are taken and requirements met

- **Rewards:** Think of how each option might compare in terms of time, cost and the final outcome. Which outcome will be closest to your desired outcome?

This part of the requirements is where you could use decision trees, cost/benefit analysis and other techniques to help you decide which option might be the best one.

Pick the best and justify your choice

Once you have all your information collected about each option select the one that is the most appropriate to use. Remember this may not be the most effective one but should be the most feasible. This means it will be the best response you can make to the challenge set given the available time, money, expertise or experience, resources or ability. The option likely to give the best result may be too expensive or take too long. This is why you need to consider the most feasible.

Collecting evidence

WHAT YOU NEED TO DO

Establish what the problem is then use appropriate ways to analyse the extent of the problem and what the features are.

Work out how you will know if or when you have solved the problem. List the standards or criteria you will use to determine whether you have been successful or not in solving the problem. Make sure others agree.

Once you are clear about what the problem is and what would be a clear proof of solving it, you then need to come up with options about how to solve it. So use appropriate ways to generate options for tackling the problem. You will need to come up with at least three options and compare the main features of each. Remember to include a comparison of the resources needed, timescales and the risk factors.

Assess which option would be the most appropriate one to use to solve the problem and be able to justify your choice. The option chosen must have the most realistic chance of success and you should explain why you think this is the best option.

Evidence requirements in a nutshell

We've talked a lot about problem solving being about bridging the gap between where you are and where you want to be in relation to the problem. This part of the evidence is about looking clearly at the problem, finding out why it is a problem and describing it clearly.

Then focus a little on the solution (where you want to be) and agree the standards or criteria you should use to show the problem has been successfully solved with appropriate people.

Now use different methods to come up with ways to solve the problem.

Take your best ideas (you need at least three), think them through, and develop them into possible options that could be used to solve the problem.

Collect as much information as you can about the feasibility and effectiveness of each option because you need to compare them to establish which is the best one. Compare them in terms of the resources each will need, the timescale each has, the risk factors involved and anything else you think is appropriate.

Once you have compared each, select the best one for you and justify the choice you made.

HINTS FOR 'EXPLORING PROBLEMS AND OPTIONS'

- Keep clear records of what the problem is
- Have a clear explanation of the scope and nature of the problem
- Keep a record of your teacher's or assessor's feedback on your evaluation criteria and how you were able to accommodate their comments
- Put your different solutions to the problem in a table to help compare one against the other more clearly
- Keep a note explaining why the methods you chose to help you come up with ways to tackle the problem were appropriate
- Hold on to records of any brainstorming, transcripts of discussions or interviews, etc.

Planning and implementing options

Planning

This is where you could use flowcharts or other techniques to help you plan. You need to draw up plans to help you solve the problem and get agreement from an appropriate person to start implementing them. Include in your planning, stages to review your progress. These can be put in after interim targets or when small tasks or objectives are due to be completed.

Plans should give details of the expected timelines and sequence of events that must take place showing key decision points. You should also consider drawing up alternative arrangements (contingency plans) just in case something unexpected happens. Good plans will have backup suggestions for resources as standby arrangements, just in case.

As a rule you should expect the unexpected, and having review stages and contingency plans thought through at the early planning stage will ensure that work goes smoothly even if you run into difficulties. Think through what could go wrong and try to create scenarios for how you will deal with these difficulties if they occur. This will help you begin to construct a contingency plan and alternative strategies for keeping the work moving forward regardless of whether you hit difficulties.

You will find out that time spent on thorough planning will make the implementation and review stages a lot easier to carry out.

Implementing

Now you can get to work implementing your plan. Get hold of the resources you need to make everything happen and then get on with it. Make sure other people involved are kept up to date of your progress and make use of appropriate people for feedback, advice and make the most of their expertise and experience to help you find an effective solution.

Monitoring and reviewing

The plan itself should be a dynamic set of arrangements that can be changed and adapted as circumstances change. Use each built-in monitoring stage as a way to review how your plan is performing, and as you learn from your experience using it, make changes to help it run more effectively.

If you created a flowchart or used timelines, keep checking progress against it as you go. This will help you ensure you keep on schedule or stick to your plan.

Try to be honest and objective about your progress and the effectiveness of your plans, and when changes are necessary make them. You can make changes because of unexpected difficulties or opportunities. This stage is really about introducing intermittent stages to check on progress and to make sure that you continue making the most appropriate decisions based on current information and experience. You need to avoid stubbornly sticking to your plan when you can adapt it to help you deal with changes more effectively.

Collecting evidence

WHAT YOU NEED TO DO

Having determined which option is the best one to solve your problem, you need to develop a plan to carry it out. Build into the plan stages to review your progress and when the plan is ready to use get agreement to go ahead from an appropriate person. Then implement your plan, making effective use of feedback and support from other people.

As you monitor and review your progress, respond to any changes by making adjustments or revising your approach.

Evidence requirements in a nutshell

This is where you put at least one of your options for solving your problem into action. You need to produce a plan of action, and get the go-ahead to implement it.

While implementing your plan use support from other people effectively and get feedback to help you find out how well you are doing.

Create time during implementation of your plan to check on your progress and revise your approach if necessary.

HINTS FOR PLANNING AND IMPLEMENTING OPTIONS

- Flowcharts can be useful touchstones to check on your progress and can be used as evidence
- Establish sources of useful feedback early on
- Don't keep people who need to know guessing

Checking your results and reviewing your approach

Checking you've solved the problem

This part of the evidence requirements is about identifying possible ways to check if the problem has been solved. This is where you could use the assessment criteria or standards you should have identified when you explored the nature of the problem early on. If you have these criteria, check that they are still relevant and use them to assess how well you have done in solving the problem.

If you don't have these criteria or assessment standards, go back and have a look at the section called 'Establishing criteria for assessing solutions' on page 103.

Before you apply your evaluation methods check that your teacher or assessor agrees that they are appropriate ways to measure your work.

Describe how well you did

Once you have identified possible methods for checking if you have solved the problem and agreed with an appropriate person that they are suitable, you need to apply them.

Once you have applied your methods for measuring your success you need to describe the results and draw conclusions from them. Your conclusions need to address how successfully the problem was solved.

Review your whole approach to finding the solution

You need to look back over your whole approach and produce an honest appraisal of how you think you did. Look at each stage in turn from exploring the problem through to your final solution. You should consider factors like those shown in the table opposite.

Choice of option for tackling problem	Planning	Resources
• How well you understood the problem's nature and extent • How effective the methods you used to find out more about the problem were • Selection methods for choosing best option • Ways of coming up with ideas about tackling the problem	• How successful the plan was • How useful contingency plans were • How well you responded to changes in circumstances • Did you make the most of any opportunities that came along? • The expected or unexpected consequences of your work	• Availability of resources • Suitability of resources • The role of other people • How effectively you used the key resources

Try to assess how well you did in each area of the work and comment on the factors that helped or hindered your progress. This is where a diary or journal would be useful to remind you of how well different aspects of the problem solving went.

Looking at the alternatives

Finally, you get a chance to use a little hindsight. Based on what you know now, say whether you think a different option or an alternative strategy for solving the problem might have given better results. Again, honesty is the best policy and you need to explain why you think other methods may have been more effective. If you end up thinking your chosen method was in fact the best way of doing things, what made it so successful? How could you improve it further?

Hindsight: the ability to understand, after something has happened

Collecting evidence

WHAT YOU NEED TO DO

You need to work with an appropriate person to establish methods you can use to check whether the problem has been solved. You then need to use these methods, draw conclusions and describe the results.

Finally, you need to review the approach taken to your whole problem-solving process. This means also assessing whether alternative methods and options might have brought better results given what you now know. Always include appropriate explanations.

Evidence requirements in a nutshell

You think you have solved the problem so you now need to:

1. Agree how you can show you have solved the problem with an appropriate person
2. Use these methods
3. Draw conclusions and describe the results
4. Assess your approach to problem solving, considering:
   – how well you think you did, and
   – whether alternative methods and options might have been more effective

---

HINTS FOR ASSESSING YOUR RESULTS AND EVALUATING YOUR APPROACH

- Identify useful evaluation criteria or methods to identify if your problem has been solved early on when you start thinking about the problem and what the solution might look like
- Don't be afraid to change how you intend to evaluate your solution to the problem
- Make sure the eventual methods you use are appropriate
- Keeping diaries or journals can be useful to remind you of how things went

---

Part 3: Opportunities

This part contains suggestions to help get you thinking about how and where you can generate key skill evidence.

At the beginning of any new course, module or unit, take some time to look at the subjects and activities you will be doing and think about how one of the key skills could help you achieve your subject goals. Be on the look-out for particular parts of your course that overlap the key skill requirements allowing you to generate evidence for both without too much extra work. When you find a relationship between a course topic or activity and the key skill evidence requirements, sketch out a few ideas and notes and discuss them with your course teacher and/or key skills assessor.

This part is split into two sections:

- **Course-related opportunities**

    The section aims to get you thinking about how to generate evidence in a wide range of courses. But don't just look at the courses you are taking! Look at the related courses for more ideas; for instance Business students should also look for ideas in Leisure and Recreation and Retail for ideas. It may even be worth looking at other courses just out of interest. This will give you more ideas about how you could generate evidence.

- **Evidence from other activities**

    This section deals with general opportunities to gather evidence that are not related to any course in particular: Creating a webpage (WWO); Producing a publication (WWO); Taking part in a club or event (WWO); Study groups (WWO); Homework and course work strategies (LP); Outward bound courses and extra-curricular activities (LP); Taking your driving theory test (LP); What do you want to do next? (PS)

Though the activities in the second section are targeted at a particular key skill some could be used for more than one key skill. For example, creating a webpage could be viewed as an opportunity for problem solving or working with others.

Course-related opportunities

Art and Design

Context

Art awards aim to combine intellectual and creative development with analytical, experimental and technical skills. They also aim to develop aesthetic understanding and critical judgement. You will work with a range of materials and develop and explore use of visual language in 2D and 3D contexts. This should provide you with a range of different opportunities to try to generate evidence for at least one of the following key skills.

Working with others

With much of the emphasis in an art course on developing an individual style and expression there may seem to be little opportunity to generate evidence for this key skill. However, there are some possibilities worth considering. The first relates to organising an exhibition of your work. Consider working with other class members to organise an exhibition or show of your final work. This is very often a feature of foundation and higher education art courses. If your place of study already plans exhibition events for art students, ask if you can become more involved in the organisation, suggesting that you would like to use this as an opportunity to generate evidence for the key skill.

Treat it like an art project itself, in that the space you choose to use should be an effective and appropriate location for the pieces. You will need to plan the event, find and organise the space, discuss how the pieces should be ordered and displayed and who should be invited.

Many art outcomes are traditionally presented in exhibitions. These can be:

- Within your school or college
- At a local venue like a community centre
- In a private space like a commercial gallery
- At an outside site or even on the Internet

The choice of locations can be conventional or perhaps a little less so. Think of how fashion shows now make use of churches, dungeons and even derelict sites like Battersea power station to show their collections. All this means organisation, and consideration of issues like:

- Cost
- Health and safety
- Security
- Permission
- Access

Presenting final work can be very stressful and there will be a lot of preparation required both at an individual level and collectively. This will provide ample opportunity to generate evidence for the key skill as you work on your own and in a group to get ready for the exhibition. The group will have to:

- Check out the venue and ensure the facilities are adequate. Look at the space, how you will use it, and the electricity supply and socket locations. Safety must be a main concern
- You will need to think through what you want to say about your work and the best words and expressions to use, either in a catalogue or when discussing it with others
- Individually you will need to think about how to draw attention to your work as well as look at all the pieces as a whole and contribute to discussion on how best to organise and arrange the displays

You will also need to work with others to produce a catalogue or guide, presentation or advertising materials, leaflets, etc.

Other 'Working with others' opportunities

- Creating a webpage for your work and the work of other students
- Organising an art appreciation society
- Working with people researching similar area of interest to get resources and discuss work in courses like 'Historical and contemporary references' (Vocational A-level)
- Study groups focused on art history or other suitable external assessment
- Working to set briefs might be a particularly good way to meet the requirements for one-to-one work

Improving own learning and performance

Personal studies and investigations

Personal studies and investigations give you the opportunity to do what you want with the media and materials you choose. You will be expected to explore and experiment with ideas, media and materials and your creative development and achievement will depend upon the quality of your exploration and research as well as your skill and your creativity. The 'Improving own learning and performance' key skill can help you organise your work, focus your efforts and give you a methodology to help you succeed in your personal studies and investigation. As you:

- Choose your media, materials, technology and equipment
- Investigate different genres, styles and techniques for your work
- Investigate the different ways to present your final outcomes

you can also generate evidence for the key skill. When you work with:

- Text and reference sources
- Specialist magazines and articles
- Original works and gallery publication
- Technical manuals or specifications
- Specialist websites and CD-ROMs

the key skill can help you use this inspiration and research effectively, focusing your effort as you aim to improve your skills. You should be able to cover the work you need to do for the key skill in your art course work, combining the two so you need to do minimal extra work. The work you will do should fall under the key skill requirements to improve your performance by 'learning through a complex practical study' or even 'further practical activity that involves independent learning'. By aligning the LP key skill with a significant area of your course and using it to develop or enhance your skills, you will be able to satisfy both the requirements for a 'substantial' example of work and 'the extended period of time'.

The LP targets you set should be art course targets and you should clear these with both your art teacher and your key skills assessor.

Other ideas:

- Working to set briefs. You can use the course targets as your LP targets. The key skill methodology will help you organise your efforts for the course work as well
- You could generate evidence for LP by looking at improving your performance through complex practical activities involving sculpture or 3D studies. Alternatively:
- 2D work could provide the focus for your LP practical activity

Problem solving

There may be an opportunity to look at tasks involving working to a set brief as an exercise in problem solving in order to fulfil the requirements of the brief. There may be further opportunities related to using computer software in different aspects of the course.

Where there are no clear problem-solving opportunities you should discuss the matter with your tutor and when you think you have a substantial art-related activity that could be suitable, clear it with your key skills assessor.

Problem solving doesn't have to be directly involved with your art learning or course work; it could relate to it in a different way. Some ideas to get you thinking:

- How to display your work on the Internet or, more generally, how to bring your work to other people's attention

- Progressing in art, e.g. getting on to a suitable foundation or higher education art course.

Business

See also: **Retail and Distributive Services**, page 172, and **Travel and Tourism**, page 179

Context
Business courses cover a range of different options and specialist areas but most have core topics to help you develop an understanding of organisations, the markets they serve, marketing strategies and some element of financial understanding and accounting. These areas will give you an opportunity to generate evidence for the key skills below.

Working with others

Marketing
If you have the chance to carry out a market research project, this provides you with the opportunity to generate WWO evidence. You should be able to agree objectives based on your intended course outcome and will have a range of issues to discuss and plan as well as different responsibilities and working arrangements to sort out. You will need to:

- Agree the market research techniques your will use
- Organise primary research methods and co-ordinate the activity allocating different roles and responsibilities
- Agree which secondary sources to use
- Agree how to analyse and discuss findings, draw conclusions and present your results

This may only be the initial stage of your WWO work because you could then go on to formulate a marketing strategy based on your results. This will mean applying the results of your market research to develop a suitable marketing strategy based on your findings.

You would thus have a 'substantial' activity that could meet requirements for each aspect of WWO.

Start by discussing your market research and marketing objectives identifying how you will generate and organise your individual and group evidence and how you will make and record decisions. The group could 'brainstorm' as a way to generate suitable ideas.

School activities
Very often business studies departments are at the centre of wider school or college student business activities. Initiatives like Young Enterprise or other business activities could be used as a way to generate WWO evidence as well. Again, like Marketing, the initiative's business objectives

can be co-opted into the key skill and the planning for the business activity can also be used as WWO evidence.

Exam preparation for finance, accounts or costing units or modules

There could be an opportunity to use WWO to organise a study group to revise a challenging subject area like the ones listed. You may be able to practise and support each other as a group, generating WWO evidence while you strengthen an area of your business work. The group could set targets and use homework, interim tests and exams as a way to evaluate performance. Meetings could be used to discuss case study work or topics that are proving to be particularly difficult.

Internal assessment projects

Business Studies courses like the A/S and A-level may have a significant amount of the final grade determined by internal assessment. Consider creating a forum that supports the group members by providing an arena to:

- Discuss their work
- Share ideas
- Seek feedback and advice
- Find support

Keep time set apart to plan and set objectives, individual responsibilities and arrangements and to discuss how the group is performing. By setting some time aside each meeting to discuss the group setup and look at the type of WWO requirements and evidence you need to create and keep, you will be able to address the key skill needs. However, the main focus is the Business.

Improving own learning and performance

Progressing on to your next course

An alternative approach involves considering what your next move is in terms of courses. What do you intend to do after you complete your Business course? If you intend to take a further Business or Business-related course (e.g. an HND or degree) you could use the LP key skill as a frame-work to help you to prepare. For example, you may want to specialise in human resources, accounting or marketing in your next course. Perhaps you have done a little amount in your current course and you think you might want to learn more about it and potentially specialise in it.

This type of approach benefits you not only by preparing you thoroughly for an important topic in your next course but also by helping you improve your chances of higher grades within your current Business course. You also get to focus your LP work on an area that obviously interests you.

Your LP aim is to extend the learning that takes place in the classroom by getting you to develop a learning and skills development programme that takes you further or deeper into the subject than perhaps your existing course requires. Make sure you discuss with your business teacher how you can set feasible targets that support, supplement and extend your course work allowing you to explore your particular interest further. Having agreed appropriate targets you can set about devising a programme making sure you work to an appropriate time frame and have a way both to measure how effectively you are learning and improving your abilities in the area and to review your progress at sensible points.

You will need to find some way to get feedback and support as well as identifying all the support and self-help materials that may be out there. This includes CD-ROMs and the Internet, which has a number of interesting specialist websites. You also need to spend time identifying an area that you are particularly interested in or will be important later. This will involve carrying out a little research into the type of content covered in the course you want to move on to. You are not aiming to meet the standard in your next course; you are trying to become more familiar with the content. The goal is to make sure you have a solid grounding in the chosen area; that way transition on to the higher course will be a little smoother and potentially easier to cope with.

Becoming more confident in a particular topic

Take time to look at the range and type of learning and content awaiting you in the business course and try to identify areas that may cause you particular problems or difficulty. You could use the areas of content you identify as the focus of your LP activity. Consider taking topics like accounting, costing, economics or finance and using one of these as the basis for LP work. These types of areas generally tend to give students the most problems and the key skill can provide a useful way to help support your course work and perhaps help you cope better with the course assessment demands.

The idea is to focus on potential problem areas early and for you to design and develop as well as implement a learning and improvement strategy to supplement and support your class work. By doing this, the problem content will be less of a threat in terms of the final assessment or your exams. By targeting an area of potential weakness, you will be improving your chances of higher grades in any assessments you do and helping to improve your confidence and command across the course.

Important in this type of approach is:

- Early and thorough exploration of the course content to identify areas of potential concern
- Clear justification to yourself and others of why the chosen area needs special attention. For example, has it caused problems in a previous course or is it completely new to you?
- Discussion of your plans with both your business teacher and key skills tutor

You can then start to work on the target-setting process, establishing timelines and identifying who could be useful sources of support and guidance. You also need to assess what self-help sources are available. Are there any

'teach yourself' books, revision guides, specialist CD-ROMs and/or specimen exam papers that can be used?

The aim is for you to devise a learning programme that supports or supplements your course work, allowing you to spend more time on a specific topic within the course content. Get your teacher to work with you to set appropriate targets and help you establish how best to support your class work.

Another important aspect of the planning will be to identify the opportunities to monitor your progress. You need to identify opportunities to use the learning and skills you are developing and get feedback on your progress. This means identifying course work occasions and internal tests or exams where you can see how much you are improving and get feedback on your progress.

This type of approach allows you to work on the key skill within the business course and, as you improve your learning or performance, generating key skill evidence, you are also improving your business work. This may eventually give you more confidence in taking the business assessments or exams.

Problem solving

Marketing

You could frame a marketing challenge as a problem-solving activity. You will certainly be able to come up with three alternative strategies to choose from and then implement the most suitable. Market research could help you establish which strategy to implement. Make sure you clear this approach with your key skills assessor. The search for an effective marketing strategy would certainly be a substantial and complex enough problem for the key skill at level 3.

Synoptic assessments

Business Studies courses include a significant amount of synoptic assessment, normally undertaken towards the end of the course. In Business Studies, synoptic assessment means being able to show that you can see the relationships between different aspects of your business course and draw together the knowledge, skills and understanding gained to tackle business issues in an integrated way. You may need to draw on all that you have learned to successfully tackle a decision-making or problem-solving exercise, deal with a case study or prepare a business plan. These are all examples of tasks that you could be set as part of your synoptic assessment.

Find out the type of synoptic assessment you will be required to do. Because it features at the end of the course you will have a chance to prepare well enough in advance. Then see if it is going to be useful as a way to generate PS evidence. Remember at this stage, the business assessment must take priority and you should use the PS only if you think there may be significant overlap or if it might be able to help you with the business work.

Impact on business of external influences

In this type of topic you could be dealing with macro and micro-economics and the legal, political and social environments in terms of their influence on business. Look to see if there will be a chance to generate PS evidence as you deal with case studies or carry out projects to try to determine cause and effect type relationships and influences of the wider socio-economic and political climate on business. PS opportunities may also occur if you will be looking at the influence of the economic policy or climate on individual businesses or business sectors. Try to focus on a specific aspect of macro-factors, and try to determine the strategic implications for businesses. Don't be too ambitious and try to focus on too much or something too general. Consider focusing on:

- Interest rates
- Exchange rates
- Oil prices
- A specific budget proposal or piece of legislation

This way you will be able to learn much more about the impact of a specific factor and its influence on business.

Construction and the Built Environment

See also: **Design and Technology**, page 121, and **Engineering**, page 124, for further ideas

Context

Construction and the Built Environment addresses issues relating to towns and cities, including the buildings and the civil engineering structures that provide their infrastructure. They also include the technology and performance of structures, buildings and services within buildings, such as water and energy supplies. You can also specialise in areas like architecture and design, building services engineering, town planning and development.

Both the core units and the specialist choices will provide you with a range of opportunities to generate evidence. Here are a few suggestions for how to use the compulsory units in the Vocational A-level to create key skill evidence. This information is designed to help you start planning and collecting the key skill evidence you need. If you are not taking the Vocational A-level, your course may nevertheless carry similar subject areas.

Working with others

Design

Units or topics that involve producing a design portfolio from a given customer brief could be used to generate evidence for the WWO group or

Opportunities

one-to-one evidence requirements. When working individually, your relationship with the customer could form the basis of the one-to-one work. If you are working in a group you could look to include a group investigation of the space and the production of exploratory sketches, drawings and associated notes as part of the WWO group objectives and responsibilities.

Area or building case studies

Consider working in small groups or even with one other to explore and collect information on an area or building you have to produce a case study for. This gives you an opportunity to address the group or one-to-one WWO evidence requirements.

Improving own learning and performance

You may want to add to the skill elements of the course by developing a higher level of ability in a specific skill area. You could use the LP key skill as a way to structure your approach and to develop a learning programme to help you achieve your goal. The skills could be in any area of construction from drawing skills to joinery. It really depends on where your interests lie.

Look to extend or further develop your skill or expertise in an area you have covered in your construction course by taking a more independent approach to your own learning. Perhaps, you have been interested in a topic that you have covered and want to take it further. It may be something that you think you would like eventually to specialise in. This would give you an opportunity to negotiate targets with your teacher or tutor and work out how best to assess how your knowledge or skills are developing.

For example, if you were interested in skill development you could look at some of the NVQ assessment standards and work towards them under appropriate supervision. You don't need to do the actual NVQ, just look at the appropriate standards and expectations and design your own learning and skills development programme around a suitable area of interest. If you are more interested in boosting your drawing skills then have a look at the appropriate British Standards that relate to drawing. The standards will give you an idea of how to assess your progress. This could be something to discuss with your teacher or tutor.

Alternatively, if your interest is in a more knowledge-based subject, perhaps because it is an area you want to go on to study at a higher level, you could build a learning programme around that. In both cases you must discuss your intentions with both your construction teacher and your key skills assessor.

Problem solving

Design

Creating a design portfolio as part of your vocational course can give you an opportunity to generate PS evidence. The work involved in appraising the use of space associated with a locality or project, interpreting a customer brief and the production of a final design solution follows the PS key skill methodology closely.

Note that the PS key skill asks for three options for solving the problem (i.e. three design proposals); this might be more than the construction evidence asks for. Look out for other differences between the two evidence demands.

Design and Technology

See also: **Engineering**, page 124, **Manufacturing**, page 157, and **Hospitality and Catering**, on page 143, for further ideas

Context
These types of courses aim to develop innovation, design capability, recognition of constraints and the ability to produce high-quality products. They provide you with the opportunity to select and apply knowledge, understanding and the skills of design and production processes to a range of technical activities. You will also be encouraged to develop a critical understanding of design and technology by drawing from contemporary and historical practices.

The exact nature of the opportunities that exist in your Design and Technology (D&T) course will depend on your chosen specialist area. Each will offer different sets of activities and circumstances that may be suited to one key skill more than another. For example, while production design of food may provide a number of WWO key skill opportunities, systems and control may be better suited to problem solving.

The guidance provided focuses on generic types of activity that should be relevant to at least two of the three focus areas in D&T.

Working with others

Design work
You may need to conduct some more detailed research to find out how best to solve a design problem or to come up with a better design solution. You could approach this task as part of a small group.

The group activity would focus on collecting appropriate information, selecting and using appropriate research techniques to use and then implementing them. Once the information has been collected, the group could become a discussion forum to discuss the information collected as well as ideas team members have relating to the actual design and what needs to go into the final design brief or specification.

This means that WWO objectives would need to focus on two group functions (collecting evidence and discussing issues). You would need to agree who does what, by when, as a group agreeing individual responsibilities as well as the group working arrangements. For the second part of the group work, objectives and responsibilities are more about active par-

ticipation and involvement in the group discussion sessions. This means not only bringing ideas and issues to discuss but also encouraging others to take part.

When you have fully discussed the information collected and all have ideas about what the design brief or specification needs to address, you can wind up the group. At this point you can all start working on the final section of the WWO evidence requirements where you review the work with others and agree ways of improving collaborative work in future. You may be able to act on these suggestions for improving the collaborative work if you work in the same group for another activity, e.g. making a product.

Making products

Whether you are involved in making a single prototype or batch production there will be an opportunity to build your WWO portfolio of evidence. It really depends on the size of the task that confronts you and the type of product you intend to make. Larger, more complex tasks will give you a better opportunity to meet more of the WWO requirements because it will be easier to have members fully involved and carrying out individual as well as group responsibilities.

In this type of activity the WWO objectives become the same as the D&T course's with regard to the actual making part of the process. You may want to set additional objectives and agree expectations for how you expect group members to conduct themselves during the course of the group work. You will also need to establish how you are going to take decisions as a group. You also need to build in some time to review your WWO and agree ways of improving collaborative work in future. This will involve:

- Agreeing how successful your work with others has been and whether the objectives have been met
- Identification of factors that influenced the outcome
- Agreeing ways of improving future group work

Large-scale projects

Many schools and colleges have a large project at some point during your course. This is either done in class time or as an extra-curricular activity. This type of activity could be a useful way to generate WWO evidence. The key skill may be a useful way to help you organise the whole project or could be used to help sort out just one particular part of it.

Improving own learning and performance

You could look to extend or further develop your skill or expertise in an area you have covered in your D&T course, taking a more independent approach to your own learning. Perhaps you have been interested in something that you have covered and want to take further and eventually specialise in. This would give you an opportunity to negotiate targets with your teacher or tutor and work out how best to assess how your knowledge or skills are developing.

For example, if you were interested in skill development you could look at some of the NVQ assessment standards and work towards some them under appropriate supervision. You don't need to do the actual NVQ, just look at the appropriate standards and expectations and design your own learning and skills development programme around a suitable section of interest. The standards will give you an idea of how to assess your progress. You could choose either a particular hand skill, manufacturing process or drawing skill to focus on.

Consider what you might like to do after your D&T course, i.e. what higher course (HNC or degree) you intend to do and try to identify an area that may be important for this next course. This could be the focus of the learning programme you devise for your LP work. Perhaps you are interested in product design or architecture. You could focus on drawing skills, looking at British Standards for ideas about what types of skills and standards are important and frame your skills development around these.

The aims are to support your class learning and to begin to focus on an area that interests you, learning more about it than may be necessary for your D&T course. You are not trying to achieve the standards in NVQs, British Standards or in your intended course. Instead you are using these as a way to find out more about the skills and start to develop some abilities in the chosen area. There may be a skill or area of interest that is just a hobby or personal interest that you want to pursue further. You can still use it as a focus for your LP work and it will still be important to find some way of measuring your progress. This is where NVQs, British Standards or some other courses could help in terms of giving you ideas to set targets and establish criteria to judge the improvements in your performance. This could be something you discuss with your teacher or tutor.

Alternatively, you may want to focus on an area of the course that causes you some difficulty and devise a learning programme to use in your LP work that supports your class work and helps you strengthen your performance. You need to discuss this approach with your D&T teacher because they can help you establish targets and devise a programme that supports what happens in the classroom, giving you more chances to practise and develop skills. You could also look at incorporating some independent learning based around self-help guides, the Internet, specialist CD-ROMs, work experience and/or advice and help from others.

Problem solving

Designing

In essence the whole process of design is a problem-solving exercise as you look to maximise the possibilities within the constraints laid down in the design brief or by the customer. Early design work will focus on exploring the nature of the problems involved in designing a suitable product and

may also involve the need to carry out research to help find appropriate solutions or ideas.

You may want to focus the PS activity on the stage before the actual realisation of designs, concentrating instead on the production of a design brief or design specification. This would be the solution to an initial design problem posed by your teacher. In this instance the option you take forward would more likely be the type of research technique you use to find out more about the design problem, allowing you to come up with the information you need to begin to create the design brief or specification.

Perhaps a more conventional approach would be to start at the design brief or specification stage for your PS work. Your final design solution would then be your PS solution and the discarded ideas would represent the options you rejected and did not take any further forward. Other issues that could also form part of the PS process include:

- Establishing the materials and components most fit for purpose
- Acknowledging the working characteristics of materials and components in your design choices
- Taking account of the restrictions imposed by tools, equipment and processes

Make sure you are clear about what is needed in the D&T work and the PS requirements before you start work. This way you can look at where there is overlap between the two activities and where the PS and D&T require different types of evidence. The PS methodology and process should fit into the type of approach you take in your design work so there may be little extra work to do. However, the PS may need you to include types of evidence that you don't need to do in your D&T work. This is most likely to happen in the final section of the PS key skill. Here you are required to apply methods to check if the problem has been solved and draw conclusions about whether it has or not. You are also required to review your approach to the problem-solving process (the design process). This includes whether you think one of your other design ideas may have been more appropriate in hindsight.

Making products
You may be able to treat the whole issue of making a product or products to meet design specifications, budgets and timelines as a logistical problem to be solved. Whether you can do this really depends on the type of product(s) you are making and the conditions and restraints that are put on the production.

Engineering

See also: **Design and Technology**, page 121, and **Manufacturing**, page 157, for further ideas

Context

Engineering courses combine a range of studies, both practical and theory and will provide you with a range of opportunities to generate evidence for all three of the key skills.

Working with others

Projects

Many courses contain projects or project units where you work in groups to design and build an engineering product of some sort. If there is no formal prescribed group work, many Engineering courses integrate different course assessment requirements into a larger piece of work.

Even if there isn't a large, integrated assignment or project to do, there might be a special project that the school or college engineering department takes part in, perhaps competing against other departments in a regional or national competition. Any of these things could be used as a focus for your WWO key skill.

You need to make sure that you are working with a group of like-minded people, motivated to do the engineering project work and meet the WWO requirements. A key part of the work will be making sure you have appropriate permission, supervision and will be working safely at all times.

Designing

You could consider generating one-to-one WWO evidence when you are designing a product as part of a customer brief. Your one-to-one would be between you as designer and the customer (the person setting the brief). See the main guidance on using design as a vehicle for WWO in the D&T guidance on page 121.

Improving own learning and performance

You could focus the key skill work either on an aspect of the study focusing on a more theoretical aspect of the course like mathematics or science topics or, alternatively, focus on a practical activity and develop particular skills.

Alternatively, you could look to extend or further develop your skill or expertise in an area you have covered in your engineering course, taking a more independent approach to your own learning. Perhaps, you have been interested in something that you have covered and want to take it further. It may be something that you think you would like to eventually specialise in. This would give you an opportunity to negotiate targets with your teacher or tutor and assess how best to assess how your knowledge or skills are developing.

For example, if you were interested in skill development you could look at some of the NVQ assessment standards and work towards them under appropriate supervision. You don't need to do the actual NVQ, just look at the appropriate standards and expectations and design your

Opportunities

own learning and skills development programme around a suitable section of interest. The standards will give you an idea of how to assess your progress. This could be something to discuss with your teacher or tutor.

Consider what you might like to do after your Engineering course. What higher course (HNC or degree) do you intend to do? Are you going to try to progress to a specialist engineering course, e.g. electronics or telecommunications? Try to identify an area that may be important for this next course and use this as the focus of the learning programme you devise for your LP work. This may lead you down a more knowledge-based route for your LP work. However, you may be interested in developing a skill further. Perhaps you are interested in product design. You could focus on drawing skills looking at British Standards for ideas about what types of skills and standards are important and frame your skill development around these.

There may be a skill or area of interest that is just a hobby or personal interest that you want to pursue further. You can still use it as a focus for your LP work and it will still be important to find some way of measuring your progress. This is where NVQs, British Standards or some other course standards could help in terms of giving you ideas to set targets and establish criteria to judge the improvements in your performance in this extension work. This could be something to discuss with your teacher or tutor.

The aim is to support your class learning and begin to focus on an area that interests you, learning more about it than may be necessary for your Engineering course. You are not trying to achieve the standards in NVQs, British Standards or your intended course. Instead you are using these as a way to find out more about the skills and starting to develop some abilities in the chosen area.

Alternatively, you may want to focus on an area of the course that causes you some difficulty and devise a learning programme to use in your LP work that supports your class work and helps you strengthen your performance. You need to discuss this approach with your Engineering teacher because they can help you establish targets and devise a programme that supports what happens in the classroom giving you more chances to practise and develop skills. You could also look at incorporating some independent learning based around self-help guides, the Internet, specialist CD-ROMs, work experience and/or advice and help from others.

Problem solving

There are a number of different areas in Engineering that provide opportunities for PS, consider:

- Designing to meet a customer brief
- Designing and making an object to meet a specification
- Mathematical engineering problems

- Scientific engineering problems
- Finding appropriate materials or alternative materials to make products
- Fault diagnosis and rectification
- Equipment or product repair

The basic design and making process of meeting a brief or specification, selecting appropriate materials and testing the end product will naturally cover all the aspects of the PS evidence requirements.

You could frame the whole issue of how to master an aspect of the course as a problem to be solved. Consider using topics like CAD or other engineering software applications as the challenge. Factor into your planning both formal class learning and your own exploratory work on the problem. Make sure you have the appropriate permission and, where necessary, supervision. You must work safely at all times.

General Studies

Context

This guidance is aimed at both the A/S and A-level General Studies courses. The range of skills the General Studies awards try to develop – for example, critical thinking and awareness of contemporary issues and evaluation – should mean opportunities to build evidence for each of the key skills. Pay attention to how your particular course is assessed.

The course may have a significant amount of internal assessment and, depending on how this is to be done, this could be a chance for you to choose a topic and try to build evidence for your General Studies course and your chosen key skill simultaneously.

Working with others

Probably the best and most straightforward way to generate WWO evidence using your General Studies course is by:

- Establishing a study group, or by
- Setting up a support and discussion group to focus on your internal assessment or project work

A study group could either focus on a particular section of the course (e.g. 'Science, Mathematics and Technology', 'Culture, Morality, Arts and Humanities', 'Society, Politics and the Economy') and could terminate when this part of the course ends. However, you could also continue the study group, moving on to another topic. Start out by focusing on a single topic area and, if the group proves to be helpful and effective, you could then agree to add to the group's remit as you go along. This way you have natural breaks where you evaluate the group performance and agree ways of improving the collaborative work to make the study group more

effective. This is an important part of the WWO evidence requirements. Try to focus on specific areas of content within the three general headings. This will allow you to develop more precise objectives.

Use major course work and class assessments as important means to gauge the progress of individuals and as a way to help you set targets and deadlines. These represent important opportunities for group members to receive feedback on their progress. This way you can measure how individuals in the study group are dealing with the topics and determine how much help the study group is for each member.

If the group is oriented more towards exam preparation, set clear revision objectives and have the topics you wish to revise discussed, agreed and then worked into your group plans. As with groups established to allow you to work with others on internal assessment or project work, the focus is on support, discussion of issues, reviewing what has been learned and helping group members to become more confident and to improve their knowledge, understanding and skills. It does not involve swapping answers. This helps no one.

Where the focus is on internal course assessment or projects, the goal is to create a forum that supports the group members by providing an arena to:

● Discuss their work
● Share ideas
● Seek feedback and advice
● Find support

Allow extra time to plan and set objectives, agree on individual responsibilities and arrangements and to discuss how the group is performing. By setting some time aside at each meeting to discuss the group setup and to look at the type of WWO requirements and evidence you need to create and keep, you will be able to address the key skill needs. However, the main focus is your General Studies course.

There is further advice about establishing study groups on page 191.

Improving own learning and performance

Take time to look at the range and type of learning and content awaiting you in the General Studies course and try to identify areas that may cause you particular problems or difficulty. You could use the areas of content you identify as the focus of your LP activity. The idea is to focus on potential problem areas early and for you to design and develop as well as implement a learning and improvement strategy to supplement and support your class work. By doing this the problem content will be less of a threat in terms of the final assessment of your exams. By targeting an area of potential weakness, you will be improving your chances of better grades in any assessments that you do and helping to improve your confidence and command across the course.

Important in this type of approach is:

- Early and thorough exploration of the course content to identify areas of potential concern
- Clear justification to yourself and to others of why the chosen area needs special attention. For example, has it caused problems in a previous course or is it completely new to you?
- Discussion of your plans with both your General Studies teacher and key skills tutor

You can then start to work on the target-setting process, establishing timelines and identifying useful sources of support and guidance. You also need to assess what self-help sources are available. Are there any 'teach yourself' books, revision guides, specialist CD-ROMs and/or specimen exam papers that can be used?

Another important aspect of the planning will be to identify the opportunities to monitor your progress. You need to identify opportunities to use the learning and skills you are developing and get feedback on your progress. This means identifying course work occasions and internal tests or exams where you can see how much you are improving and get feedback on your progress.

Instead of focusing on areas of content that may cause problems, an alternative approach would be to concentrate on an area of general studies that could feature heavily in any future course you may want to take or supports another course you are taking. This approach depends on how clear you are about what your next move is in terms of course progression, i.e. which Higher National or Degree course you intend to take, and being able to investigate which content may be particularly relevant. All this preparation work and investigation is not wasted effort because it can all be used as evidence of the planning and target-setting process in your LP key skill.

Problem solving

One of the intentions of the General Studies syllabus is to encourage you to think critically, logically and constructively about significant problems and to develop an appreciation of the strengths and limitations of different approaches to show that you have an ability to justify your own approach. This means that there will be opportunities during your course to generate PS evidence.

Look carefully across the main content categories within your General Studies courses and try to identify where the best opportunities for PS work can be found. You should be able to identify potential opportunities in:

- Science, Mathematics and Technology
- Culture, Morality, Arts and Humanities
- Society, Politics and the Economy

Within each of these syllabus areas there will be a number of different opportunities to generate PS evidence. You may find it useful to look at

the guidance given for other qualifications to help you identify suitable opportunities for PS. For example, the Mathematics and Science guidance may help you with this part of your General Studies, while Art and Health and Social Care may have useful guidance for dealing with the 'Culture, Morality, Arts and Humanities' section of your syllabus. There will be other course guidance you may also be able to use.

Within the three syllabus areas identified above you may find the following types of topics particularly useful in generating PS evidence:

- *For Science, Mathematics and Technology*
  - Mathematical reasoning and its application
  - Understanding of scientific methods, principles, criteria and their application
- *Culture, Morality, Arts and Humanities*
  - Creativity and innovation
  - Beliefs, values and moral reasoning
  - Media and communication
- *Society, Politics and the Economy*
  - Explanation and evaluation of human behaviour
  - Relationships between law, culture and ethics
  - Ideologies and values in society

Synoptic assessment (the ability to show you can draw together knowledge, skills and understanding from across the course) will be an important feature in General Studies. Your course will feature a significant level of synoptic assessment towards the end of the course. Find out how your particular General Studies syllabus will deal with the synoptic assessment because this may also create opportunities for PS evidence. This is because one of the possible ways in which synoptic assessment might be carried out may be through some form of assignment that requires you to research or investigate an issue or problem drawing on knowledge, understanding and skills acquired and developed during the course.

Even if the final assessment of this aspect of the course is external (i.e. in the form of an exam) there will be teaching, skills development and rehearsal in your class work as you prepare. Here you may have an opportunity to combine this work with your PS requirements.

The other main PS opportunity may come with your internal assessment (the project or investigation you may have to do that will count towards your final overall grade). The internal assessment may count towards as much as 30% of your final grade so you will certainly have a substantial enough block of time and significant enough activity to work with. You may find that because much of this has to be done independently the PS key skill can give you a useful framework and methodology for approaching it. This way you can organise you work and efforts more effectively while at the same time generating your PS evidence.

Geography

See also: **Travel and Tourism**, page 179, for further ideas

Context

The range of knowledge, skills and understanding associated with Geography should provide ample opportunity to incorporate key skills into your studies. The breadth of the physical and human syllabus components and the challenges of fieldwork surrounding the personal enquiry and environmental investigation should provide opportunities to practice 'Working with others', 'Improving own learning and performance' and 'Problem solving'.

Working with others

Fieldwork

Most Geography courses put some emphasis on investigative work, based on evidence collected from primary and secondary sources. Fieldwork will be an important part of the process of collecting information. Carrying out fieldwork will give you a chance to generate WWO evidence. Look at this as an opportunity to build your key skill portfolio without having to do too much additional work.

Although the interpretation and analysis of the results will probably have to be done individually, you could work with small groups to organise and carry out the fieldwork and to reflect on the results. This type of approach may help you make sure that you prepare properly, making the most of the opportunity by collecting the information you need as part of an effective team. The team can them provide you with a useful forum to discuss the findings and reflect on the working methods and the group performance.

You could work with others to collect the fieldwork evidence for the group and then discuss the findings later collectively. You can then concentrate on interpreting the results and writing up your project or personal enquiry on your own. You could use the group as a 'sounding board' as you work.

This type of approach provides you with an opportunity to get the most out of the fieldwork experience giving you a chance to discuss ideas about the most appropriate methods and techniques to use and the various types of quantitative and qualitative evidence. This may lead to a more thorough appreciation of the issues by individual group members.

If working in a group on a series of fieldwork tasks conducted over a period of time (these could be related to the same or different projects), you can review the group performance and how decisions are taken. This will help you address the final section of the WWO key skill that focuses on reviewing your work with others and agreeing ways of improving collaborative work in future.

WWO objectives and decision taking will need to address:

- Where to collect evidence
- When to collect evidence
- What evidence to collect (e.g. primary, secondary; quantitative and qualitative)
- How to collect evidence, i.e. what techniques to use
- Who does what
- How to report and discuss findings

Improving own learning and performance

Progressing on to your next course

If you intend to progress on to a more specialist Geography-related course either at HND or degree level consider using the LP key skill as a way of improving your knowledge, skills and understanding of a topic that will be important in your future course. For example, you may want to specialise in cartography or geology in your next course. Perhaps you have done a little in your current course and you think you might want to learn more about it and potentially specialise in it.

This type of approach benefits you not only by preparing you thoroughly for an important topic in your next course, but also by helping you improve your chances of better grades within your current Geography course. You also get to focus your LP work on an area that obviously interests you.

Your LP aim is to extend the learning that takes place in the classroom by getting you to develop a learning and skills programme that takes you further or deeper into the subject than perhaps your existing course requires. Make sure you discuss with your geography teacher how you can set feasible targets that support, supplement and extend your course work allowing you to explore your particular interest further. Having agreed appropriate targets you can set about devising a programme. Make sure you work to an appropriate time frame and have a way of measuring the effectiveness of your learning. Show you can review your progress at sensible intervals.

You will need to find some way to get feedback and support as well as identifying all the support and self-help materials that may be out there. This includes CD-ROMs and the Internet (which has a number of interesting specialist websites).

You also need to spend time identifying the topic area that you are particularly interested in or which will be important later. This will involve carrying out a little research into the type of content covered in the course you want to move on to. You are not aiming to meet the standard in your next course, you are trying to become more familiar with some of the content. The goal is to make sure you have a solid grounding in the chosen area, that way transition on to the higher course will be a little smoother and potentially easier to cope with.

Becoming more confident in a particular topic

Take time to look at the range and type of learning and content awaiting you in the Geography course and try to identify areas that may cause you particular problems or difficulty. You could use the area of content you identify as the focus of your LP activity. The idea is to focus on potential problem areas early and for you to design and develop, as well as implement, a learning and improvement strategy to support your class work. By doing this, the problem content will be less of a threat in terms of the final assessment or your exams. By targeting an area of potential weakness, you will be improving your chances of better grades in any assessments you do and helping to improve your confidence and command across the course.

Important in this type of approach is:

- Early and thorough exploration of the course content to identify areas of potential concern
- Clear justification to yourself and others of why the chosen area needs special attention. For example, has it caused problems in a previous course or is it because it is completely new to you?
- Discussion of your plans with both your geography teacher and key skills tutor

Then start to work on the target-setting process, establishing timelines and identifying useful sources of support and guidance. You also need to assess what self-help sources are available. Are there any 'teach yourself' books, revision guides, specialist CD-ROMs and/or specimen exam papers that can be used?

An important aspect of the planning process will be the identification of opportunities to monitor your progress. You need to identify opportunities to use the learning and skills you are developing and get feedback on your progress. This means identifying course work occasions and internal tests or exams where you can judge how much your performance is improving and get feedback on your progress.

Problem solving

Some Geography syllabuses and assessment may involve decision-making, problem-solving and/or evaluation exercises. In order to successfully complete these types of exercises you will need to draw together relevant knowledge, understanding and skills learned in different parts of the course to tackle decisions, problems or issues that may be new to you.

SYNOPTIC ASSESSMENT

Synoptic assessment is a type of assessment that needs you to draw together knowledge, skills and understanding from across your entire course to help you deal with the questions or exercises set.

This type of approach is seen as an acceptable example of synoptic assessment. There will be a significant amount of synoptic assessment taking place in your Geography assessment. Try to establish what type of

synoptic assessment takes place in your particular course and whether or not this could be a useful way to generate PS evidence.

Applied geographical skills

There is a clear link between the types of approaches you will be asked to take when applying geographical skills and the methodology and requirements laid out in the PS specifications. As you develop and apply geographical skills (perhaps as part of fieldwork or as a part of your personal enquiry exercise) you will:

- Collect, handle and interpret primary and secondary data
- Recognise potential relationships, problems and hypotheses
- Select and use sampling techniques (random, systematic and statistical)
- Acknowledge the limitations of data collection methods
- Summarise data and reach conclusions

These types of skills and activities can be fitted into a PS approach to a geography issue. For example, as you recognise potential relationships, problems or hypotheses, you will also be exploring a complex problem. The options you need to come up with to solve the problem could be the different data collection and sampling techniques you could use to generate the information you need. You can use your knowledge of research to select an appropriate technique or sampling methods to take forward, be able to justify your choice and plan how to use it effectively. You will also be able to judge how successful your chosen methods were and discuss whether the alternative methods you dismissed may have given better results.

As you can see there should be little additional work needed to cover the PS key skill requirements if you are able to frame your fieldwork, personal enquiry, investigation or other use of applied geographical skills in the context of a problem to be solved or hypothesis to be tested.

Graphic representations

The whole issue of how to represent something graphically could be presented in a problem-solving context. Firstly, you will need to explore how to represent the chosen subject. This means looking at the various:

- Graphic forms
- Cartographic forms
- Tabular forms

After having chosen the most appropriate method to use there will be range of smaller issues and more detailed decisions to make before you decide upon exactly how something could be represented in your chosen method.

Analysis and evaluation of evidence

Having collected data as a result of fieldwork, the PS opportunities continue as you decide how best to analyse it. Your Geography course may expect you to be able to apply the following statistical techniques at a basic level:

- Data description in terms of normal distribution, mean, mode, median, standard deviation, and/or
- Analysis of relationships using statistical techniques like Spearman's rank correlation and chi squared (χ^2)

By looking at the range of statistical techniques available and choosing the technique most appropriate, applying it and reviewing it accordingly, you could be addressing aspects of the PS key skill.

The whole process of collecting data to help you find out more about your observations or hypothesis begins to address the first section of the PS requirements. In this section you explore a complex problem (your observation or hypothesis). Selection of an appropriate fieldwork technique or method could start to address the PS requirements about selecting one option and taking it forward to help solve the problem.

Alternatively, you could use the selection and use of an appropriate statistical technique or techniques to meet the 'choosing and implementing an option' part of the PS requirements. If you need to do both as part of the Geography work, then use both in the key skill as well. This way you will have more to review, discuss and comment on when you address the last part of the key skill.

Other problem-solving opportunities

There may be opportunities to generate evidence in topics involving data analysis, fieldwork or in more practically focused topics. Look for PS chances in topics like:

- Rural and urban planning
- Population changes and trends
- Coastal and river management
- Environmental investigation
- Managing environments

Health and Social Care

Context

Although there are a number of opportunities in the compulsory sections of Health and Social Care courses like the Vocational A-level, remember to look at the possibilities that exist in your optional choices. There will be a number of different opportunities throughout the course to target each of the three key skills while also generating your vocational evidence. Try not to be too ambitious and attempt too much. Though there may be the chance to generate evidence for more than one key skill, think carefully about whether you will be able to handle the extra organisation and effort that this would involve. Make sure that whatever you choose to do your vocational work does not suffer.

If you start early enough and look at the range of topics to be covered during your entire course, you will be able to identify the best opportunities for generating evidence for both the key skill and Health and Social Care simultaneously. Your course will be long enough to allow you to address more than one key skill. Try to plan how to sequence each key skill and complete one before you start on another. Avoid having too many conflicting and competing demands at the same time.

Working with others

There will be a number of opportunities to address both the group and one-to-one aspects of the WWO evidence requirements in Health and Social Care. Topics where you may find the best opportunities include those listed below.

Equal opportunities and clients' rights

You may need to explore the promotion of clients' rights and provision for the protection for vulnerable clients in a health, social care or early years setting. This type of activity may be an opportunity to work in small groups to collect information on your chosen area.

If this topic was to be the subject of external assessment then it could be the focus for WWO evidence by setting up a study group.

Communicating in health and social care

Look carefully at vocational evidence requirements that ask you to work with different client groups in one-to-one interactions and group interactions. This might be your best chance to use the same evidence for both the vocational and WWO requirements. Look carefully at both sets of demands and discuss with your teacher how best to use this type of topic as a vehicle for your WWO evidence.

Health, social care and early years services

You may be asked to investigate a local health, social care or early years organisation. This will give you a chance to work in a small group to collect the appropriate information and carry out any necessary research. Set your WWO targets by looking at the vocational requirements and identifying the types of information you need to collect. Then you can start allocating roles and responsibilities and setting timelines.

You can extend the WWO activity to include discussion of your research results. Although the vocational requirements will probably demand that you interpret and act on this information on your own, you will be able to discuss ideas and issues within your group. Successful and effective discussion of the information in a well-organised and disciplined manner could also be set as a target for your WWO.

Factors affecting human growth and development

This type of topic might be a useful focus for a study and revision group. You should be able to identify clear targets and topics for discussion for the group and be able to plan the areas that you want to discuss well in advance. Look at the course delivery or teacher timetable for the unit and use this as a way to set your study group timetable and plans. Establishing a clear agenda for group meetings and giving group members early notification of discussion topics will mean that people should be able to prepare for the meetings and come with issues to discuss or questions to ask.

Remember to build in ways for the group to assess how well or effectively they are learning. Use course work requirements as a way of monitoring and reviewing both the individual member's performance and the effectiveness of the group in helping members improve.

Research perspectives in health and social care

Consider setting up a discussion forum where group members update each other on the progress made in their individual projects and talk about related issues and methodology. Have the potential group members think carefully about what in the objectives should be discussed at the initial meeting. Remember to set objectives relating to your vocational work as well as the workings and performance of the group, for example an objective about having informative meetings where everyone plays an active part in discussions. Ask that everyone also set personal objectives that fit with the collective ones, to encourage them to contribute effectively and value the contribution of others.

Improving own learning and performance

Factors affecting human growth and development

This is a useful topic to use as a focus for LP work. This is because it requires a substantial amount of learning and may well be assessed externally. Try not to be too ambitious by targeting the whole subject or a large section of it. Instead, look at the unit closely and select a smaller topic that may be particularly challenging or seem difficult to grasp and use this as the focus of your LP work.

The LP requirements can help you to devise an independent learning programme to support and complement your class work, helping you to more fully understand your chosen topic. This has the benefit of not only helping you to meet the LP requirements with a suitable level of challenge over an appropriate length of time, but also helping you prepare to meet the demands of the vocational assessment.

Your goal will be to increase your confidence and ability in the content area chosen by developing a learning programme to supplement and support your class work, thus helping you tackle the potentially problematic area. The key is to devise a learning strategy that will support your class work, allowing you to take a greater degree of responsibility and control over this aspect of your learning.

Look at the vocational course and the timetable used by your teacher to help you develop an appropriate timeline and targets for the LP work. Try to identify early on where the opportunities to test your knowledge are by using course work, class tests or projects. Discuss this strategy with your vocational teachers and ask their advice on issues like:

- Setting appropriate targets and objectives
- How to assess your improving knowledge, i.e. setting interim and final targets
- How to tie in the LP work to support your Health and Social Care course
- Working out a suitable time frame

Communicating in health and social care

If you are not using this type of topic as a chance to generate WWO evidence or communication key skill evidence, perhaps because you don't feel confident enough yet, then consider using it as a focus for LP work. Your focus would be to improve your communication skills in one-to-one and/or group interaction. You would set yourself a range of different targets involving different methods of communication. Areas to consider as possible targets include:

- Being more confident or less nervous in group situations
- Learning to use enhancing factors more effectively in communication and minimising the presence of inhibiting factors in your communication
- Improving your use of body language and non-verbal communication
- Improving your presentational skills

These are just a few suggestions to get you thinking about possible targets. You also need to consider how you can self-assess and use peers to assess your performance. This means establishing who would be most appropriate to use as a source of feedback. You may also want to consider using audio or video equipment as a possible means to help with your self-assessment. Consider these issues when you work on developing a strategy to assess how much progress is being made and to help you identify where you may need to improve further.

You may be able to use the successful completion of your vocational work relating to communication as proof of your meeting your LP targets if you frame them in an appropriate way.

Problem solving

When it comes to PS in your health and social care work, you need to try to look for opportunities that involve dealing with unknown situations or with difficulties that mean applying your knowledge and trying out a range of techniques or skills. This could be in a variety of settings and could involve:

- Trying to establish an effective communication strategy when dealing with a difficult client or sensitive issue
- Establishing an effective strategy for determining the physiological status for an individual
- Working out the relationship between homeostatic mechanisms involved in controlling the physiological factors using primary and secondary sources of data

- Deciding how access to a particular service or range of services could be improved
- Establishing and testing criteria to determine the effectiveness of a particular service or piece of legislation, code of practice or charter

There are a number of difficult (sometimes contentious) and competing issues and interests in the health and social care arena. For example, provision and funding of services can be politically charged and disputed at local and national levels. There may also be opportunities to generate problem-solving evidence when discussing, learning and then applying your knowledge, skills and understanding of the following issues and topics:

- What actually constitutes health and social care
- Tensions between private and public provision
- The role of insurance
- Means-testing
- Changes from the internal market to integrated care

Either through actual case studies, simulation or role playing, there may be an opportunity to develop and test your problem-solving abilities as you:

- Try to resolve disputes
- Balance budgets
- Put forward suggestions about how best to maintain or improve levels of care provision

It may well be possible for your teacher to set a problem-solving issue in a health and social care setting, perhaps in a local context, allowing you to apply the knowledge, skills and understanding you have acquired in your course. This will help you to understand this learning in an applied context and real (or simulated) life setting, while also allowing you to generate evidence for problem solving.

History

Context
A/S and A-level History courses will encourage you to develop skills that allow you to:

- Analyse, evaluate, interpret and use historical sources of different kinds
- Use a range of historical concepts in appropriate ways, for example, in discussing or presenting a case, argument or account
- Communicate clear, concise and logical arguments substantiated by relevant evidence

As you learn to develop these types of skills and abilities in class, and practise them in preparation for exams, you will also have an

opportunity to generate sufficient evidence to allow you to attain a key skill. Pay particular attention to how your course is assessed. More specifically, look to see how much internal assessment there might be. Your internal assessment could be in the form of a personal study, historical investigation or assignment and represents a good opportunity to generate key skill evidence.

Working with others

History discussion or support groups

One obvious way to work on WWO is to set up a small discussion group with others taking your course. The group can act as a forum to discuss different aspects of the course and talk through issues relating to projects or homework. This way the group has a dual purpose and group objectives should be drawn up to reflect this. For the WWO, subject-related objectives can be based around the syllabus content, or the areas you choose to focus on. Time-related objectives could take their lead from homework and assessment requirements.

The group needs to be run as a semi-formal affair with time spent preparing a schedule of topics to discuss. Members will need to take responsibility to lead off discussion on different topics during meetings, and if members are not leading at a particular meeting then they need to come prepared to take part in informed discussions. Build these suggestions into individual targets as you allocate roles and responsibilities.

The group will also need to organise a venue, schedule of topics and a timetable that acknowledges any deadlines for assessments. Remember that your aim is to create a forum to encourage people to communicate clear, concise and logical arguments, discussing the evidence that substantiates or supports different points of view. In order for this type of group to succeed the individual members will need to be comfortable in each other's company, so choose your group members carefully. They should also have a strong interest in the subject and be committed to making it work.

Don't make the group a chore, keep it relaxed and supportive. To help you do this also discuss the practicalities involved with the course and talk through any issues and uncertainties you have concerning course work, projects, final assessments and exam preparation. You can also include which resources to use, where and how to get the right books and how you can pool resources. If the group turns out to be an effective way to reinforce your course learning and is a useful forum to discuss history, consider extending the remit to include exam preparation.

Don't rush to complete the WWO, let the group run its course and gradually build up your portfolio as you go. You will have time to review the success of the group after the history exam and monitor your progress at convenient points (like half-term and end of term). Individual members can gauge the usefulness of the group by looking at their performance in class and how they perform in homework assignments and projects.

Collecting and analysing historical information

You will probably be required to investigate specific historical questions, problems or issues. Depending on the nature of the topic and the amount of information you need to gather and interpret, you may be able to generate WWO evidence as you go. Ideally, you would work with a partner in a one-to-one context or with a small group.

Make your WWO objectives the same as the course objectives focusing them on the collection and analysis of information. Then add in some objectives relating to your group aspirations (i.e. how you should work together).

Improving own learning and performance

Investigating your own history syllabus

History is a dynamic and controversial discipline, though its may not seem so at times. Controversy has often involved the following types of issues or claims:

● History has been recorded only by the winners of conflicts
● History has been written and recorded by men
● Some historical accounts are written with a European bias (Euro-centric)

You will spend a lot of time learning about the use of historical information and sources and learning how to analyse, evaluate and interpret historical accounts, sources and texts. Why not turn these techniques around and apply them on a section of your own course. In a sense, the part of the syllabus that outlines the content you need to cover relates to a period of time or theme, makes a statement about what is important about that particular part of history. It presents the knowledge and understanding related to a particular period or historical theme that it sees as worthy of your attention. But what is the syllabus not getting you to look at that was also happening at the time? What is the syllabus not asking you to learn about?

Consider carrying out a critical evaluation of a particular section of your own History syllabus (a specific module, or part thereof, for example) as a way of applying the evaluation and analysis skills you are developing and as a way to generate LP evidence. You are attempting to step back from your own course, evaluating it as statement of what is important during a certain historical period or episode.

You will need to devise a learning programme based around doing some wider reading about the period or historical theme you choose to help you put your course in some sort of context. A simple and straight-forward starting point might be to look at the syllabus from different examination boards and compare how they cover the same historical period or event. What are the differences?

Alternatively, you can choose to focus your critique on a particular investigative theme. For example, you can look to see how it addresses the role of women during the period. Start by becoming familiar with the

whole area of feminist critique, it may be completely new to you and you may find it interesting. This could be an interesting way of extending your learning about the different types of evaluation and analysis within history as a field. Alternatively, you could focus on different cultural or religious groups that appear to be absent from the syllabus, finding out more about them during the period you cover in the course.

How you choose to carry out your investigation and evaluation really depends on the content area you select. You could focus on:

- Women
- Cultural or religious minorities
- Indigenous peoples

The risk with this type of evaluation is that it gets complicated very quickly. To keep you on track and focused, and to prevent your getting in too deep, consider answering one of the following questions (or something similar):

- How does the content seen as important for a particular historical period or episode in your syllabus compare with other syllabuses and/or historical accounts?
- What was happening within a particular section of society (chosen by you) that doesn't seem to feature in the syllabus learning relating to a particular historical period or episode?

As a result of each of these activities, you will have sufficient information to evaluate how the period or historical theme was presented by your course syllabus.

You will need to discuss this type of approach with your History teacher, asking advice on how to set suitable learning targets. You also need to ask them for a copy of your course syllabus. You also need to establish:

- How you will get hold of the other examination board syllabuses
- What other resources you may need
- What time frame you should work to
- How you will monitor and review your performance

The results of your investigation could either be:

- Shared with others as a presentation
- Discussed with your teacher
- Written up as a brief proposal to your exam board
- Written up as a brief report

The bigger picture
There may be a specific country, part of the world or people that you are particularly interested in not addressed by your History course. If so, then consider devising your own learning programme to allow you to investigate your area of particular interest. Looking at what was happening in your chosen country or area while you also cover your History syllabus will give you an interesting comparative perspective.

Alternatively, you could focus on several countries and as you learn about a particular historical period or theme in your course you could research what was happening at this time in your chosen countries. You won't need to go into much detail about any one particular country. The point is to build up a comparative profile of activity across a small range of countries to help you put your course work in perspective. At the same time, you would be applying your research and investigative skills and generating LP evidence.

Problem solving

Internal assessment

The personal study, individual assignment or historical investigation that you need to do as part of your internal assessment may be a good way to generate PS evidence. Very often internal assessment focuses on investigating specific historical questions, problems or issues. You should always choose the particular topic for your assessment based on an area that interests you most and don't be tempted to try to force the PS key skill into the work. Once you have decided on a topic see if there is any way that the PS key skill requirements could also be addressed.

Discuss your intentions with your History teacher and key skills tutor. If you do decide to combine the two then use the History deadlines to help establish a time frame for the PS also. But remember that you can always go back to the PS work so your History work must take precedence.

Other problem solving opportunities

Further opportunities to generate evidence for PS could exist in A/S and A-level courses when you:

- Study change over a period of time and try to determine or analyse its causes and consequences
- Explore and understand the significance of particular historical events, individuals, issues and societies.
- Use historical sources, accounts, arguments and interpretations to help you explain and make judgements

Look carefully at the areas of your syllabus that address these types of activities and see if any can be used as an opportunity to generate PS evidence.

Hospitality and Catering

Context

Although there are a number of opportunities in the compulsory aspects of Hospitality and Catering courses like the Vocational A-level, remember to also look at the possibilities that exist in your optional choices. You may find that it makes sense to combine different aspects of the course

(e.g. a compulsory part of the course with one of your optional choices or two or more compulsory aspects) to generate your key skill evidence. Alternatively, you may be able to generate sufficient evidence from a single occasion. The secret will be to identify early on where the opportunities may exist in your Hospitality and Catering course.

Working with others

In Hospitality and Catering there will be a chance to carry out large- and small-scale investigations into a range of different topics. Look for opportunities in topics about:

- **Purchasing, costing and control**
  You might have to conduct research into the purchasing cycle procedures and into how costs and prices of products and services are prepared, presented, monitored and controlled.

- **The hospitality and catering industry**
  You may be asked to investigate the importance of the industry nationally, employment patterns or particular organisations and outlets.

- **Food and drink operations**
  Investigation of preparation, cooking and serving of menu items.

- **Accommodation and front office operations**
  This type of topic may mean investigating and carrying out research into facilities, products and services provided by accommodation and front office operations as well as looking into the influence of environmental and technological changes.

- **Customer care**
  This may involve an investigation into quality service standards.

- **Safety, security and the environment**
  This type of topic may involve investigations into hazards, controls, monitoring and review procedures as well as having to carry out risk assessments.

The types of investigation listed above are probably most effectively done in smaller groups and should focus on the collection and discussion of information. You will be expected to analyse and interpret the information yourself in order to meet the vocational evidence requirements so concentrate the WWO efforts on activities that can be done in groups. Clear your intended approach with your vocational and key skills teachers.

You may want to link the investigation and research work for two or three different topics, bringing them together as one more extensive investigative activity to help you better meet the WWO requirements. This really depends upon the range of topics you are studying. Other topics like 'Safety, security and the environment' may have sufficient group work opportunities to be the sole focus of your WWO efforts. Either way, plan your approach carefully and discuss your intentions with appropriate people.

You will find that the WWO structure and methodology can help you organise your research and investigation work more effectively and will encourage you to think more about the process of collecting information.

Make sure that by doing some of the hospitality and catering work in a group you are not excluding yourself from meeting certain higher grade requirements. Check carefully what the higher grading requirements are, establishing the degree of independence you need to show in order to meet the higher grades. This way you will stop the WWO work's conflicting with the grading requirements of the Hospitality and Catering unit.

Other main opportunities to generate WWO evidence will occur when you work in groups to provide some sort of catering service. There will be optional units available that will give you a chance to combine the food production and service and the WWO requirements. You will also be able to combine performing front office services as part of a team in a similar way. Regardless of whether the activity is simulated or real-life, you should still be able to look for an opportunity to combine your vocational work with WWO.

Improving own learning and performance

Skills development

There will be a range of skills (especially in catering) that may be appropriate in a number of hospitality topics. The development and improvement of each skill provides a possible focus for LP activity. You will need to identify the units that feature the specific skill you want to focus on and then build these units into your planning for LP. Each unit may give you an opportunity to assess and determine how your are improving and will help you generate LP evidence. Hopefully, the evidence that involves your using the particular skills can be used for the vocational and key skill evidence.

This type of approach will certainly involve taking an extended period of time because you will be drawing on evidence generated in more than one unit.

External assessment topics

You should consider focusing on a key topic for external assessment and use this as the focus of an LP learning programme. By tackling a more difficult subject area in this manner you might be able to build confidence and ability in an area that may otherwise cause you problems. The LP learning programme will get you to set targets to show that you can deal with the subject and get you working towards dealing with your problems. The LP key skill will encourage you to check your understanding by looking for ways to apply what you have learned and by getting you to check your understanding with others.

Establish early on in your course which units are to be externally assessed, then spend time looking at the knowledge, skills and

understanding that will be covered. Try then to identify an aspect of the content that may be more problematic for you and use this as your focus. Try not to choose something that you are able to cope with comfortably. You are trying to take some of the pressure off your vocational external assessment by tackling any potential problem area early on. Look at the content and see if there is anything that has caused you difficulty in the past. If so, you can start your LP work by trying to establish what the particular problem has been. Otherwise, look for an area that might be totally new to you and that you are not sure about.

Your goal will be to increase your confidence and ability in your chosen content area by developing a learning programme to supplement your class work thus helping you tackle any problems you have. The key is to devise a learning programme that will support your class work allowing you to take a greater degree of responsibility and control over this aspect of your learning.

Discuss this strategy with your vocational teachers and ask their advice on issues like:

- Setting appropriate targets and objectives
- How to assess your improving knowledge, i.e. setting interim and final targets
- How to tie in the LP work to support your Hospitality and Catering work
- Working out a suitable time frame

Problem solving

Safety, security and the environment

There could be an opportunity to generate PS evidence by using this type of unit as a focus. You could set the task of 'how to produce a thorough assessment of hospitality and catering workplaces' as your goal and then use the learning, experience and activities you carry out in the vocational unit to help you generate the evidence. Review the results of your risk assessments, interviews with various staff and the methods you used to investigate hazards, controls, and monitoring and review procedures. With hindsight, you can then try to come up with an effective 'blueprint' for assessing health and safety, food safety and security in hospitality and catering workplaces.

Look carefully at the PS requirements and see how you can fit them together with your Hospitality and Catering vocational requirements.

Food production

The preparation and production of a range of balanced, nutritional meals to budgets or other constraints like time could be viewed in a PS context. The logistical issues involved in running a catering facility could also be framed in a PS context.

Information and Communications Technology

Context

Regardless of whether you are taking the A-level, A/S level, Vocational A-level or some other Information and Communications Technology (ICT) course there will be a range of different opportunities to build a portfolio of evidence for each one of the three key skills. Start the process by looking at the type of content you will cover, the activities you will perform and the type of assessment you will be required to do. Then you can establish where the best opportunities exist to generate evidence for your particular key skill.

Working with others

There are a number of different types of activity in ICT courses that could be used to generate WWO evidence. Listed below are a few examples of activities to get you thinking about how you can use your own particular course to generate WWO evidence. Start the whole process by looking at the types of topics, activities and projects you will be doing during your course and identify where the best opportunities lie. Ideally, you want to find opportunities to generate your course and key skill evidence at the same time.

Spreadsheet solutions

You may have to come up with a spreadsheet solution to meet specified requirements or given customer needs. This activity may even include the production of user documentation. This is an opportunity to develop one-to-one types of WWO evidence as you work with the potential customer or eventual user to establish how best to meet their needs. Your teacher could take the role of customer. You will need to liaise closely with them to establish how best to produce clear and effective support documentation.

Programs to meet user needs

The course may require you to create working programs to meet user needs as well as supplying user support documentation. This is another opportunity to generate one-to-one type WWO evidence. There will be opportunities to involve the user in different stages of the design and testing process ensuring that the program(s) eventually meet their needs. Each time you meet to discuss something this gives you an opportunity to develop and refine your programming and related documentation, to tailor each to address their needs. It also represents a chance to maintain your co-operative working relationships over an extended period of time and to agree changes to achieve your objectives. This is an important aspect of the WWO evidence requirements.

Keep in mind that while your course is concerned with a functioning program accompanied by appropriate support documentation, the key skill is more concerned with your demonstrating that you can work effectively in a one-to-one context. Remember this when you generate your WWO evidence.

System installation and configuration

Look for opportunities to work in a small team to design, configure and install an IT system and operational system. The WWO objectives and timelines would be the same as those set for the IT activity and as a group you will need to establish individual responsibilities and working arrangements. This should be a good opportunity to generate some of the evidence required for the IT course and WWO simultaneously.

Internal assessment and course-work projects

Most Information and Communications Technology courses have a substantial amount of the final grade based on internal assessment. Find out exactly how much of your final grade is based on internal assessment and what form this assessment is expected to take. It could represent a good opportunity to generate WWO evidence. Though you may not want, need to or be allowed to involve others in the actual production of your work, you could set up a small support group and discussion forum. This would allow you to:

- Discuss your ideas with your peers
- Discuss aspects of the course
- Give and receive feedback
- Practise presenting your work
- Work out organisational and presentational issues

If you adopt this type of approach you will need a clear remit (and objectives) for the group as well as a plan showing how you will use the group throughout the duration of the internal assessment work or project. You will also need to establish individual responsibilities and working arrangements. The WWO work will need to focus more on the organisation and effective running of the group than on the IT work itself.

Improving own learning and performance

One way to generate evidence for the LP key skill while supporting and improving your class work is to target a particular syllabus area and make it the focus of your LP activity. Choose any area that may need additional attention and devise a set of targets and a plan to implement them in the form of a programme to improve your learning and performance in that particular area.

Take time to look at the range and type of learning and content involved in the area you choose. Try to identify areas that may cause you particular problems or difficulty. These could become the focus of your LP activity. The idea is to focus on potential problem areas early and for you to design and develop as well as implement a learning and improvement strategy to supplement and support your class work. By doing this, the problem content will be less of a threat in terms of the final assessment or your exams. By targeting an area of potential weakness, you will be improving your chances of higher grades in any future assessments and helping to improve your confidence and command across the course.

Important in this type of approach is:

- Early and thorough exploration of the course content to identify areas of potential concern
- Clear justification to yourself and to others of why the chosen area needs special attention. For example, has it caused problems in a previous course or is it completely new to you?
- Discussion of your plans with both your ICT teacher and key skills tutor

You can then start to work on the target-setting process, establishing time-lines and identifying useful sources of support and guidance. You also need to assess what self-help sources are available. Are there any 'teach yourself' books, revision guides, specialist language CD-ROMs, websites and/or specimen exam papers that can be used ?

If you are more confident in a particular aspect of the course perhaps you might want to devise a plan to extend your learning and improve your performance in a particular area. This may be a useful way to help you improve your chances of higher grades in any exam or assessment you do. You can discuss with your ICT teacher how to develop a wider range of IT skills and/or how to explore topics or areas in more depth. Once you have agreed suitable targets, you can start devising a learning programme. You might have a specific interest in a particular type of IT-related issue, e.g. webpage design, or you may know that a particular area of content will be important in a course you want to do in future. For example, if you are planning to go on to study a specific type of software engineering there may be a particular area of programming that it is important to master or at least have a solid grounding in. This approach really depends on being clear about what your next move is in terms of course progression (i.e. which Higher National or degree course you intend to take), and being able to investigate the content which may be particularly relevant. All this preparation work and investigation is not wasted effort because it can all be used as evidence of the planning and target-setting process in your LP key skill.

Problem solving

PS is an integral part of most Information and Communications Technology courses and there should be plenty of opportunities to generate appropriate evidence. For example, much of the internal assessment will be about showing you can address a problem and demonstrate that you can analyse, design, implement, test and evaluate systems. You may also have to apply the principles of problem solving using computers to demonstrate the techniques of system documentation and development. If

so, this represents a great opportunity to address many of the PS key skill requirements while working towards your internal assessment requirements. In fact, the PS key skill may help you develop a methodology to use in your course work when tackling the internal assessment component of your course.

Look carefully at the type of activity you select for the internal assessment and try to identify where the overlap with the PS lies. This will help you establish any additional work that needs to be done to fully address the key skill evidence requirements.

Most ICT courses have as an aim the need to encourage you to develop an understanding of the main principles involved in solving problems using computers. This means that there should be sufficient opportunity to generate evidence for your PS portfolio in other aspects of the course as well, namely:

- In developing an understanding of the main principles of system analysis and design, methods of problem formulation and planning for solutions using computers
- In developing a systematic approach to problem solving within the context of software
- When applying the analytical skills, you will need to learn how to judge the feasibility of computer-based solutions to problems
- When designing solutions, this will also involve developing the ability to evaluate alternative proposals and solutions (an important aspect of the PS requirements)

You will also be expected to develop the knowledge, skills and understanding to determine the effectiveness of solutions to specific problems. This is a good opportunity to address the PS requirement to check, describe and review the approaches taken.

Very often, the assessment objectives in your course will involve trying to determine how well you can:

- Analyse a problem and identify the parts which are appropriate for a computer-based solution
- Select, justify and implement appropriate techniques and principles to develop data structures and algorithms for the solution of problems
- Design, implement and document an effective solution using appropriate hardware and software

Land and Environment

Context

The guidance provided looks at opportunities to generate evidence for 'Working with others', 'Improving own learning and performance' and 'Problem solving' within the compulsory sections of the course. If you go on to specialise in a particular area, e.g. plants or animals, and take other units you will find that further opportunities arise. Weigh up where the best opportunities are for you, i.e. where evidence for both courses can be worked on simultaneously, and try to exploit these if you can.

Working with others

Natural resources of the land and environment sector

When it comes to reporting on the natural resources available to a business organisation you may have to undertake an initial investigation of the business. The vocational evidence or learning demands may ask you to find out accurate information about the business's products (goods and/or services), its location and how production relates to the business's use of resources. You could make the collection of information the focus of your WWO activity, extending it to include the collection of evidence about how the company conserves, manages and modifies resources and how its activities affect the landscape. This type of investigative activity gives you an opportunity to work with a partner in a one-to-one situation, in a small group context (or both), focusing on gathering information about the company and its activities. For example, discuss how the group can focus on collecting business information and data, then discuss breaking the group into pairs to work on a particular aspect of the research and investigation. When it comes to doing the soil analysis, researching weather records or looking at the impact on the landscape, everybody could work in pairs. This means you can use this particular type of unit to meet both aspects of the WWO requirements.

Make sure you discuss this approach with your teacher and look at how it might affect the vocational requirements for higher grades before you start anything. For example, to get a higher grade you may have to work independently.

So WWO work would centre on planning how to collect information on a business organisation's:

- Products
- Location
- Use of resources (soil, climate, water, energy, etc.)
- Conservation, management of resources and environmental policies
- Influence on the environment

You then need to frame these as objectives for the WWO requirements and establish appropriate working arrangements and responsibilities. Consider exploring all the avenues for finding out information on the company, perhaps allocating different methods or sources of information to individuals. For example, there will be the company's own literature, its website, the local press archives (often held in the local library) just to get you started. You can do a search on the Internet under the company name to see what other information may exist.

Consider setting a little time aside to do a survey of local opinion and attitudes about the business in relation to an issue in the unit. This may give you some insight into the perceptions of the local population, helping you develop a more complex appreciation of the issues.

COURSE-RELATED OPPORTUNITIES | **151**

Discussing what you poll opinion on and how best to do it, designing a suitable questionnaire, then analysing and presenting the results will also help you generate WWO evidence and may help you achieve higher vocational grades. The WWO will certainly help you develop effective plans.

Ecosystems

There may be an opportunity to work with others to collect primary research data on the identification and location of species. The WWO focus could be on agreeing objectives, planning, conducting, and finally analysing and discussing this data as a group. You will be expected to interpret the data individually, but you should be able to discuss your findings with the group. Once you have a rough idea of what you would like to do and what the central objectives would be, discuss them with your course and key skills supervisors before going any further.

Remember that the data will be the focus of the land and environment effort; the effectiveness of how you work together, organise, carry out responsibilities and working arrangements will be the focus of the WWO.

Improving own learning and performance

Natural resources of the land and environment sector

See the guidance offered above in the WWO section because much of it is the same for LP. If you decide to use this type of topic as the focus for LP then take time to look at some of the higher-grade requirements in the vocational unit as well. You can use LP to help you develop an effective plan and it can help you perform research independently in an organised and well-thought-out manner. By getting you to think about the work involved in the unit, it may also help you present your final information in a logical and well-structured manner.

Once you have looked at the Land and Environment requirements and the LP requirements, draw up some initial ideas for targets and discuss these with appropriate people. Your key skill assessor and vocational course teacher would be obvious starting points. Then you can firm up your targets based on their suggestions.

This type of activity involves a mixture of practical and study-based work that includes independent learning. The task will also be substantial enough to meet the requirement and may also take an extended period of time.

Set clear targets for your vocational work, and develop a plan and time frame for achieving these targets. Assess what information you need and determine where this information could be found. Try to explore the full range of possible sources of relevant information. Set targets that not only deal with collecting appropriate information but also relate to mastering the technical language of the area.

Your goal is to take greater responsibility for your own work and to show independence and the ability to manage your work by taking responsibility for your own investigation. Monitoring and reviewing your progress will be important, this is why you need a clear and comprehensive plan to help ensure you meet your targets. Build in at least two review stages (consider one at the end and one at a suitable interim stage) and evaluate the different strategies you chose to adopt. Don't be afraid to make any changes if you think they will help you meet your targets. Remember to explain the changes you make.

Problem solving

Plant management

There is an opportunity to generate evidence for PS when it comes to looking at the effects of environmental conditions and nutrition on healthy growth of plants. You may have to make connections with commercial practice, environmental conditions and nutrition provided and the structure and function of the plants themselves. This may mean some investigation and even some practical work that could become the focus of PS activity. The PS can help you carry out this work, by encouraging you to develop a logical approach to the task, and help you create a well-structured methodology to tackle the research and experimentation.

By looking at the PS requirements early on in the vocational course you will see that there is a chance to generate evidence that can be used for both the PS and Land and Environment without the need to do too much extra for the key skill. In order to fully meet the PS requirements, you may have to look at what the relationship might be between commercial practice, environmental conditions, the nutrition provided and the plant biology. Develop a simple hypothesis to test, then test it in a simple, small-scale manner. Though this might mean more work in addition to the basic vocational evidence requirements, showing this degree of insight, independence and initiative may mean not only that you meet most of the PS requirements but also that you meet some of the Land and Environment higher grade requirements.

Environmental analysis

You may have to conduct an environmental impact analysis or some other form of analysis that could also become the focus of PS activity.

Taking the environmental impact analysis as an example, you could look to use PS as a way to help you organise and structure your thoughts in terms of how to plan and carry out the analysis and how to identify suitable criteria to use in the evaluation.

PS can be used to help you formulate effective plans, justify your ideas and conclusions and can help guide you through the work, helping you to work, more independently.

Focus on the issue of how to make an effective analysis of a business organisation in terms of its environmental impact and come up with three possible criteria or indicators that could be used. Assess which one is the most effective. Alternatively, develop you own ideas about the steps a company could take to improve its environmental performance and explore them, then decide which would have the greatest environmental benefit. By working through this type of process you can not only explore aspects of the vocational work but also begin to meet the PS requirements.

Leisure and Recreation

See also: **Business**, page 115, and **Travel and Tourism**, page 179, for further ideas

Context

Leisure and Recreation courses cover a range of different core subjects and will include opportunities to specialise in areas of particular interest. Take time to get a clear picture of the range of different subjects that you cover and find out a little about each. Then you can look at which units give you the best opportunities to generate key skill evidence. Once you have looked at the suggestions below, you should also look at the guidance in related courses like Business and Travel and Tourism.

Working with others

Leisure and recreation in action

At some point in your Leisure and Recreation course you will get a chance to plan an event or to carry out a team project. Look for opportunities to work in a group when producing and implementing a business plan for either the event or project. Business plan objectives can be turned into some of your WWO objectives as well. For WWO your intended outcomes would be a logical and coherent business plan, a successfully executed team project or event and effective working arrangements and relationships. These may also be aspects of the vocational course requirements.

Other areas of overlap that may produce evidence capable of being used in both your vocational course and your WWO portfolio of evidence include:

- Effective planning throughout the project, keeping appropriate records of all team meetings
- Specifying objectives and establishing individual roles and responsibilities
- Consideration of resource needs (physical, human, financial), legal obligations and timescales
- Effective participation in running the project
- Keeping records of your own individual contribution
- Analysis of your own and the team's performance

Look carefully at the overlap and differences in the two sets of evidence requirements (Leisure and Recreation and WWO) and discuss with your team the work that can be used for both and the extra work that may need to be done for each.

Keep in mind the evidence of your own individual contributions that will need to appear in both portfolios as well as the collectively generated evidence. You also have a chance to meet the WWO requirements as an effective, supportive and considerate team player and thus also begin to meet some of the vocational higher grade requirements. Identify the possibilities for meeting the higher vocational grades early and factor these into your own personal WWO plans and objectives.

The WWO can help provide a useful framework for holding your vocational teamwork together. This probably represents your best opportunity in Leisure and Recreation to generate WWO evidence without having to do too much additional work. Just be careful about subtle differences in the two sets of evidence requirements. In fact this could be a useful topic for discussion for an early group meeting.

Keep talking to both your Leisure and Recreation teacher and your WWO assessor to make sure you are on the right tracks with both sets of work.

Safe working practices

If you have to assess how leisure and recreation facilities or events manage their health, safety and security responsibilities and how they meet relevant legislation and regulations to ensure a safe working environment, consider working with another person. Alternatively, you could work with a small group to visit a site, interview appropriate individuals, carry out research and discuss findings. Either way you could use this type of topic to address the one-to-one or group WWO requirements.

The sports industry

Consider working with a small group of people that share a common interest in a particular sports industry so as to investigate:

- The scale, economic importance, the organisation and funding of the sport
- The importance of the mass media
- Major trends in the sport

Consider allocating different sources of information to different group members so that each person can bring back what they find and add it to the information gathered by the rest of the group. To do this effectively, you will need to discuss exactly what and how much information you will need. Tell everyone to record how and where they found the information so that others can explore the sources further if they wish.

The WWO work should really be restricted to gathering evidence and discussions of the information you find. You will be expected to produce an individual assessment of the sport for your vocational course. Before embarking on this type of activity discuss with the other group members and your teachers whether you think you are able to generate sufficient evidence for the key skill.

Marketing

If the emphasis in your marketing course or unit is on actually creating marketing strategies and carrying out market research, consider using this as an opportunity for generating WWO evidence. Look at the advice given in the Business course guide, page 115.

Improving own learning and performance

Marketing

If the course aims to help you develop an understanding of how UK Leisure and Recreation uses marketing then you may find that you can use this as an LP focus. Don't choose to learn about marketing generally as your target, focus on something a little more specific. Consider a narrower topic like the marketing mix, and think about using the following suggestions to help you frame your targets:

- Understanding the marketing mix and the technical terms associated with it
- The strengths and weaknesses of marketing mixes
- The relationship between marketing mix and market research

When you establish your LP targets look carefully at the vocational evidence requirements and even the appropriate higher-grade evidence requirements and try to create a coherent set of LP targets around a key part of the course. You may want to focus on reinforcing the learning contained in your marketing course or extend your knowledge of an aspect of the course with some additional learning of your own.

Supporting your course work or pursuing an area of interest

You can reinforce your course work and the related learning by creating personalised learning targets and goals. These can be developed into your own learning programme. If the aim is to extend your knowledge and understanding then work with your teacher to establish some more ambitious targets that allow you to get deeper into a subject than perhaps the course allows. Either approach will suit the LP key skill.

By really getting to grips with a challenging area of content you can build confidence and be better prepared for any assessment you may have to do. You can use the LP key skill to devise a personal learning programme, setting targets to help you improve your performance in a specific area of the course. The aim is to support your normal course and class work, not replace it, so consult your teacher and get advice on how to set appropriate targets and feasible goals.

Alternatively, if you are coping well with the course demands why not use the LP key skill to develop a learning programme that could extend your knowledge, skills and understanding in a specific area of Leisure and Recreation. By digging deeper into a specific area of interest you may either cover some useful groundwork for a higher course you intend to do, or you may improve your chances to get higher grades in your current course.

If you know the course you want to take next (i.e. an HND, or even degree) consider looking at the types of content that will feature heavily in the first term or year of the course and choose an aspect of it to find out more about. You are not trying to meet the higher standards of the course through your LP work; rather, you are devising a learning programme based on doing some background preparation, making sure you have a good grounding in the content area. This may make the transition on to the course a little smoother. If you don't want to take this type of approach then just choose a topic within your current course that you are particularly interested in and want to pursue further on your own.

You need to consider what additional resources you can use. There may be self-help books, CD-ROMs or websites that you can use. You also need to find ways to monitor and review your progress. Make sure your Leisure and Recreation teacher and your LP assessor are happy with your targets and your extra work.

Problem solving

Marketing

The whole issue of determining how effectively businesses use marketing could be set in a PS context. Working out how successful or effective a marketing strategy is for a company could be an exercise in detection, investigation and research.

SWOT and PEST analyses could become activities to help you find out more about marketing and business and could be used in both your vocational course and your WWO portfolio of evidence. You could either look at a particular type of marketing generally, e.g. the effectiveness of the Internet as an advertising agent, or look at the strategy of one company in particular, producing an appraisal of the company's marketing strategy. The PS key skill could help you by providing a useful methodology and framework to help you focus your efforts. This type of activity could also be a useful way of reinforcing your vocational learning and worthwhile preparation for an external assessment involving marketing.

Manufacturing

See also: **Design and Technology**, page 121, and **Engineering**, page 124, for further ideas

Context

The Manufacturing awards cover a range of topics; the compulsory units give you a broad understanding of some fundamentals and the optional units are slightly more specialised. Both can be used to generate key skill evidence. It is worth learning a little about each of the units in order to build up a picture of where your opportunities to generate key skill evidence may come from.

Here are a few suggestions for how to use the compulsory units in the Vocational A-level to create key skill evidence. This information is designed to help you start planning and collecting the key skill evidence you need. If you are not taking the Vocational A-level, your particular course may carry similar subject areas.

Working with others

Working effectively in teams is an essential part of the manufacturing and production process, so there should be a number of opportunities to generate evidence for this key skill. Look especially to the 'Product design and creation' type units as well as units like 'Manufacturing products'.

The 'Manufacturing products' unit in the Vocational A-level may well ask you to work in teams and produce evidence of team meetings. This will mean you have a chance to generate vocational and key skill evidence concurrently. You should be able to align:

- The manufacturing targets and the WWO objectives
- Your manufacturing and WWO responsibilities
- Your manufacturing and WWO working arrangements

Be careful that you don't overlook vocational or WWO evidence requirements. You will find that the vocational unit may ask you to produce:

- Process flowcharts
- Production plans and schedules
- Records of team meetings that you need to create to show how tasks were allocated, how progress was monitored, how problems were dealt with and how improvements were made

These can also be used in your WWO portfolio of evidence. This, along with similar production units, will be your best chance to generate vocational and WWO evidence simultaneously without having to do too much additional work. You may even find that the WWO key skill methodology will help you meet some of the higher grade criteria in the manufacturing unit.

Design

Units or topics that involve producing a design portfolio from a given customer brief could be used to generate evidence for the WWO group or one-to-one evidence requirements. When working individually, your relationship with the customer could form the basis of the one-to-one work. If you are working in a group you could look to include market research, the analysis of the data you collect as a result of this research, the creation of design specifications, proposals and final solutions as part of the WWO group objectives and responsibilities.

Improving own learning and performance

Topics like quality assurance and control may be new to you. They become increasingly significant the deeper you go into manufacturing as a discipline. They play an important part in Higher National and degree courses and if you want to progress in Manufacturing you really need to understand the knowledge and skills related to quality assurance and control. Because they are so important and probably new topics to you, consider making them a special focus using the LP key skill to really get to grips with the neccesary information.

You can use a mixture of formal classes and personal learning to research and learn more about the discipline. By using further, independent study you can aim to get a good, solid grounding that will pay off in helping you to succeed in your vocational assessment as well as generating evidence for the key skill. Choosing a topic like quality assurance and control to use as the focus for your LP key skill work has the following advantages:

- It provides you with a suitable and substantial challenge that will benefit your vocational work
- It is certainly a complex enough area and is clearly at an appropriate degree of difficulty
- It uses a combination of study-based and practical activities
- It is an area of central importance for all types of manufacturing (food, textile, chemical and heavy engineering)

You may even find that taking a personal interest in these subjects helps you achieve some of the higher grades in the relevant Manufacturing unit. You can even set some of the grading criteria listed in courses like the Manufacturing Vocational A-level as targets for your LP work.

In creating your targets for the LP key skill, try to align them as closely as you can to the vocational evidence requirements so you have less work to do across both courses.

You don't have to use the ideas above just for quality assurance and control. You can use them for any topic. However, you should try to choose a subject less familiar to you or one that causes you a little difficulty. This way you will really feel challenged and have more to gain by doing well, i.e. success in the key skill and in your Manufacturing course. Use the LP key skill as a way of addressing an area of weakness and pick up some extra credit along the way.

Problem solving

Design units also provide a great opportunity to address the PS key skill. How to fulfil the customer brief to the satisfaction of the customer becomes your complex problem. Creating different design proposals based on the design specification and then finally selecting and implementing the most feasible would then become the focus of your activity.

The vocational assessment requirements for design have a clear relationship with the PS key skill requirements and you should be able to work on both simultaneously without adding too much to your workload. The same evidence you generate for the design unit will also be useful for your PS key skill portfolio.

Other design-related requirements that will also be useful in helping you meet the PS requirements include:

- Describing and prioritising manufacturing constraints

- Choosing suitable materials and manufacturing processes
- Selecting a final design solution from your design proposals
- Reviewing your design work and approach

The PS key skill will help you approach the whole design issue systematically and can help you plan and organise the vocational work more effectively. This may help you meet some of the higher grade requirements in your design unit. Note that the PS key skill asks for three options for solving the problem (i.e. three design proposals); this might be more than the Manufacturing evidence asks for. Look out for other slight differences in evidence demands.

Mathematics

Context

It may not always be obvious how you can address the WWO, LP and PS key skills within your Mathematics course. However, don't just look for opportunities to generate evidence using the mathematics work, also consider how you can generate evidence by looking at how you can approach the work and how you can organise yourself to do the work or to prepare for mathematics assessments.

Spend time discussing with your Mathematics teacher and your key skills tutor where you think the opportunities are and ask for any thoughts they have on how best to proceed.

Working with others

Probably the best and most straightforward way to generate WWO evidence using your Mathematics course is by:

- Establishing a study group with others taking the same course, or by
- Setting up a support and discussion group to focus on your internal assessment or project work

A study group could focus on a particular section of the course (e.g. trigonometry, calculus) and could be ended when this part of the course is complete. Alternatively, you could set up a group with a longer-lasting purpose, changing the topic focus as you cover different aspects of the Mathematics course. Start out by looking to focus on a single topic area and if the group proves helpful and effective, you could then agree to add to the group's remit as you go along. This way you have natural breaks where you evaluate the group's performance and agree ways of improving the collaborative work to make the study group more effective. This is an important part of the WWO evidence requirements.

Use major course work and class assessments as important means to gauge the progress of individuals and as a way to help you set targets and deadlines. These represent important opportunities for group members to receive feedback on their progress. This way you can measure how individuals in the study group are dealing with the topics and determine how much each member is benefiting.

If the group is oriented more towards exam preparation, set clear revision objectives and have the topics you wish to revise discussed, agreed and then worked into your group plans. The focus is on support, discussion of issues, reviewing what has been learned, helping group members to become more confident and to improve their knowledge, skills and understanding of mathematics. It does not involve swapping answers.

Where the focus is on internal course assessment or project work the goal is to create a group that supports group members by providing a forum to:

- Discuss their work
- Share ideas
- Seek feedback and advice
- Find support

Allocate time to plan and set objectives, to identify individual responsibilities and working arrangements and to discuss how the group is performing. Though the focus is mathematics, you still need to deal with the issues involved in keeping the group focused and successful. By setting some time aside each meeting to discuss the group setup and look at the type of WWO evidence requirements, you will be able to address the key skill needs.

You can find further guidance about establishing study groups on page 191.

Improving own learning and performance

Take time to look at the type of learning and content awaiting you in the Mathematics course and try to identify areas that may cause you particular problems or difficulty. The areas you identify could become the focus of your LP activity. The idea is to address potential problem areas early and for you to design and develop (as well as implement) a learning and improvement strategy to supplement and support your class work. By doing this the problem content will be less of a threat in terms of the final assessment or your exams. By targeting an area of potential weakness, you will be improving your chances of higher grades in any assessments you do and helping to improve your confidence and command across the course.

Important in this type of approach is:

- Early and thorough exploration of the course content to identify areas of potential concern
- Clear justification to yourself and to others of why the chosen area needs special attention; for example, has it caused problems in a previous course or is it completely new to you?
- Discussion of your plans with both your Mathematics teacher and key skills tutor

You can then start to work on the target-setting process, establishing timelines and identifying who could be useful sources of support and guidance.

You also need to assess what self-help resources are available. Are there any 'teach yourself' books, revision guides, specialist CD-ROMs and/or specimen exam papers that can be used?

Another important aspect of the planning will be to identify the opportunities to monitor your progress. You need to identify opportunities to use the learning and skills you are developing and get feedback on your progress. This means identifying course work occasions and internal tests or exams where you can see how much you are improving and get feedback on your progress.

Instead of focusing on areas of content that may cause problems, an alternative approach would be to concentrate on an area of mathematics that could feature heavily in any future course you may be taking. For example, if you are planning to go on to study a specific type of engineering there may be a particular area of mathematics that it is important to master. This approach really depends on being clear about what your next move is in terms of course progression, i.e. which Higher National or degree course you intend to take, and being able to investigate which mathematics content may be particularly relevant. All this preparation work and investigation is not wasted effort because it can all be used as evidence of the planning and target-setting process in your LP key skill.

Problem solving

Regardless of the particular syllabus being followed you will be encouraged to learn how to represent situations mathematically, understand the relationship between real-world problems and standard and other mathematical models and identify how these can be refined and improved. You need to identify where this type of activity takes place in your course and decide how you can use it to help you generate PS evidence. (This may be the best or clearest opportunity to generate evidence for PS.)

Another clear opportunity to generate PS evidence, where you are able to have more influence over the mathematics topics and approach, is the internal assessment that you may have to do as part of the final course assessment. You are looking for chances to apply your mathematical knowledge, skills and understanding to real-life problem-solving contexts. This will give you an opportunity to develop evidence for your internal assessment and PS key skill simultaneously. The PS key skill may also provide you with a work methodology that will help you cope better with the demands of internal assessment.

Media

Context
Though different media courses may cover a range of different content and specialise in different forms of media, most are built around key areas

like understanding media texts, media production and marketing. Take a little time to look at the types of topic you will cover and try to identify early on how you could use these topics to help you generate evidence for your chosen key skill.

Working with others

Developing media proposals

Developing media proposals could either become the basis for your WWO activity on its own or could be part of a larger WWO focus that included developing proposals and producing media artefacts. The proposal itself represents a piece of work that is both substantial and complex enough to be suitable for the WWO evidence.

By focusing your WWO work on the proposal, you have the option to continue the group effort into the production stages if you wish or if you don't have sufficient WWO evidence. You could use the natural break that occurs after the proposal is finished to evaluate your group performance and review how you could improve making your team more effective. Consider keeping things simple at first by using the proposal work as the focus and build from there, if necessary.

The main WWO work objective for the group would be the same as your Media course objectives, for example developing a proposal for a media artefact that shows you are able to develop ideas and conduct appropriate research.

As a group, you then need to discuss:

- The type of artefact you intend to make
- The different objectives and timelines
- Your individual and collective responsibilities
- The different working arrangements
- The type of research you need to do
- How to take decisions
- The constraints that confront you

Marketing strategies

Your Media course may require you to create a marketing strategy for a new or existing media product. This could provide you with an opportunity to work in a group and generate evidence for WWO. You could focus the group activity on carrying research on audiences and competitors, collectively carrying out primary and secondary research. Once you have generated the research information you could discuss it as a group and discuss how successful you were as a group. At this point, you could work individually to produce your own marketing strategy based on the information collected.

Producing media artefacts

When you have to produce a media product, you will probably have to work in teams. This provides you with a natural opportunity to also create

evidence for WWO. You will have to set clear objectives for your production based on careful planning and research and also establish the different team roles. You can also use this type of evidence for your key skill portfolio.

The vocational course may also ask you to:

- Produce evidence showing your input into the research and planning
- Produce records of your roles and responsibilities
- Produce evidence of your production and post-production responsibilities
- Evaluate how you performed and carried out your responsibilities as well as commenting on the team performance

All this work can also be used as evidence in your WWO. If you intend to use production units as a source of evidence for WWO take time to look at both sets of evidence requirements and make sure you are clear about where they overlap and where they differ. This way you will be clear about what needs to be done for both.

Improving own learning and performance

Working on your production skills
Developing media production skills would certainly be a complex enough practical activity that would give you the chance to provide substantial evidence of meeting the LP requirements over an extended period of time.

As you assess your skill level, you can set yourself some targets and challenges then plan how to meet these using support from appropriate people. You are really devising a learning programme for yourself, so you need to work out what skills you want to improve, how you can develop these skills and the criteria you will use to demonstrate you have achieved this higher skill level.

You could focus the LP activity on a new skill or look to build on something you are learning to do as part of your Media course. Then the focus would be to take your skill levels to a higher level as a result of independent learning. Make sure you discuss any plans with both your Media teacher and your key skills assessor. Both need to agree that your plan to target and improve an aspect of your production skill is appropriate.

You may want to address something more study based. Consider working independently to extend your knowledge and understanding of media analysis. You could focus on furthering your knowledge of elements of text, narrative or representation issues or any other aspect that particularly interests you. You could devise a learning programme for yourself, setting challenging but realistic targets. This might be particularly useful in helping you to reinforce learning in an area that could feature in external assessments or it could help you gain a greater familiarity and grounding in the area if you intend to study it at a higher level.

By pursuing your own area of interest independently you also begin to develop a higher level of knowledge and insight into the area and have something interesting to discuss or report at interviews for places on

Media courses. The LP key skill can help you organise your efforts and pull them together in a clear and coherent manner, helping you to organise an effective learning programme for yourself.

Problem solving

Marketing strategies

Perhaps you prefer to work on marketing by yourself. You still have an opportunity to generate evidence for the PS key skill. You could frame the whole issue of producing a marketing strategy for a new or existing media product as a problem. You could then carry out your own research and use it to generate three possible strategies based on your findings. After further research and deliberation you can decide which is the best one to take forward.

Producing media artefacts

There could be the opportunity to present the production of a quality media product that meets the timelines, budget and other constraints as a problem. You should discuss this approach with your Media tutor and your key skills supervisor before getting started just to make sure both are happy with this approach.

Modern Foreign Languages

Context

The following guidance is designed to apply to all Modern Foreign Language (MFL) courses. Hopefully it will help you start to think about how to use your particular language studies to find opportunities to generate evidence for a key skill. However, you need to spend time becoming familiar with your own particular course requirements, the nature and amount of internal assessment, e.g. projects that count towards your final grades, and the types of language-related activities offered by your college or school.

Working with others

There are three main areas to look for opportunities to generate WWO evidence in any MFL course, these are:

- Through the internal assessment part of the course
- Organisation of a study or discussion group
- Particular activities or events organised through the school or college

Internal assessment

Consider setting up a small support group of friends or colleagues as a forum to discuss ideas and issues related to the internal assessment requirements of your course. Group members could report progress and

discuss how to organise, carry out and present the work, dealing with issues and supporting each other. The timelines for your group plans would be based on the timelines for your assessment. If you think this might be a useful way to deal with the language internal assessment requirements, look at the guidance about forming study groups on pages 191–3.

DEFINITIONS

- **Internal assessment:** the work you will do that counts towards your final grade during your course.
- **External assessment:** the exam, test or other form of assessment set by your awarding body and normally taken at the end of your course or unit

---

Study or discussion groups

Consider setting up a small group to focus on developing and practising your speaking. The group aim would be to work on your manipulation of the MFL accurately to help you organise facts and ideas, present explanations, opinions and information. The main consideration in setting up your group is to choose people that you will be comfortable working with. You should not feel embarrassed or awkward. Try to create a group where people have roughly the same standard of language skills. This may make it easier for everyone to keep track of discussions.

If you don't feel confident enough about setting up a discussion-type group, then use the culture of the country as a focus. Your MFL course may expect you to develop knowledge of the culture of countries where the language is spoken. This means learning about, among other things, literature or lifestyle.

Look carefully at the course requirements and try to identify early on how you could use this type of approach to help you practise and improve your language skills. The intention would be to support your class work, so involve your teacher, ask for advice and feedback on your ideas.

Activities or events organised through the school or college

Many schools or colleges organise trips to the country whose language you are studying. Not only does this help you apply and improve your language skills, it also gives you insight into and contact with the contemporary society, culture and heritage of the countries in which your MFL is spoken. Alternatively, opportunities to generate WWO evidence may centre on the organisation of a social or cultural event rather than an overseas trip. Either way, there is still an opportunity to get involved in the organisation of the 'French trip' or 'Greek night' at your school or college and use them as a vehicle for generating WWO evidence.

If no such opportunity exists, discuss the possibility of running a social evening with a theme that relates to the countries or people whose language you are studying. This will give you ample opportunity to generate both sufficient and appropriate evidence. Make sure you look at the 'Running an event' guidance to find further help.

Improving own learning and performance

Generally speaking, most MFL courses will address the following four areas:

- Speaking
- Reading and listening
- Writing
- A cultural component

One way to generate evidence for the LP key skill while supporting and improving your class work is to target one of these four areas and make it the focus of your LP activity. Choose any area that may need additional attention and devise a set of targets to improve your learning and performance in that particular area.

Take time to look at the range and type of learning and content involved and try to identify areas that may cause you particular problems or difficulty. You could use the areas of content you identify to become the focus of your LP activity. The idea is to focus on potential problem areas early and for you to develop as well as implement a learning and improvement strategy to supplement and support your class work. By doing this, the problem content will be less of a threat in terms of the final assessment or your exams. By targeting an area of potential weakness, you will be improving your chances of higher grades in any assessments that you do and helping to improve your confidence and command across the course.

Important in this type of approach is:

- Early and thorough exploration of the course content to identify areas of potential concern
- Clear justification to yourself and others of why the chosen area needs special attention; for example, has it caused problems in a previous course or is it completely new to you?
- Discussion of your plans with both your MFL teacher and key skills tutor

You can then start to work on the target-setting process, establishing timelines and identifying useful sources of support and guidance. You also need to assess what self-help sources are available. Are there any 'teach yourself' books, revision guides, specialist language CD-ROMs, websites and/or specimen exam papers that can be used?

If you are more confident in a particular aspect of the course, perhaps you might want to devise a plan to extend your learning and improve your performance. This may be a useful way to help you improve your chances of better grades in any exam or assessment you do. You can discuss with your language teacher how to develop a wider

range of language skills and/or how to explore topics or areas in more depth. Once you have agreed suitable targets, you can start devising a learning programme.

Problem solving

It is not always easy to see how PS can be readily done alongside your MFL course without creating either too much additional work or by making the whole process a little contrived and artificial. Both ways will detract from the benefit and enjoyment of doing the key skill and, if at all possible, you should avoid this type of situation. However, that still leaves the problem of how to generate evidence for your PS portfolio using your MFL course. It will be important to discuss the possibilities with both your MFL teacher and your key skills tutor.

That said, here are a few ideas to help get you thinking about how to generate relevant PS evidence. Firstly, rather than using the organisation of a school or college trip or a social event like a cultural evening as an opportunity to do the WWO key skill, either could be used as a chance to generate evidence for PS. If a trip is involved, perhaps finding the money to pay for it is the problem you need to solve.

Another idea would be to target an area of the course that you find difficult and try to devise a way to become more confident or proficient in the area. Although parallel to the ideas and methodology behind the LP key skill, there may be an opportunity to approach the whole matter in a problem-solving vein. You would need to take the issue of finding an effective way to learn and improve your skills in the specific area as the problem and try out alternative methods and learning techniques. This type of approach will involve a lot of consultation and discussion with your MFL teacher because you do not want to cut across any teaching that takes place during the course. The idea is to try out other techniques and methods in your own time and see if they can be used to support or supplement the learning that takes place in the classroom.

Performing Arts

Context

Opportunities to generate key skill evidence for 'Working with others', and 'Improving own learning and performance' and 'Problem solving' will exist throughout your Performing Arts course. There will even be occasions when some topics or units could be used to generate more than one key skill. However, try not to be too ambitious and remember the more you take on the harder you will need to work to organise your evidence. At the same time you must ensure your vocational course requirements don't suffer as a result of your key skill work. Aim to identify specific topics that provide the best opportunities to generate vocational and key skill evidence simultaneously and complete one key skill before embarking on another. Though you don't have to do it this way, it may be easier to organise your work and keep focused on the key skill and your Performing Arts evidence.

Working with others

Historical and contemporary contexts

If you are given the task of investigating the development of a particular art form, consider establishing a small team of people interested in the same art form to work together collecting information and discussing the findings and issues. Using a specific period of history may be an alternative way to focus your group, with members interested in different art forms.

The main focus of the work would involve research and the collection of information with interpretation of the information and the use of the group as a forum for discussion and presentation of ideas being the subsequent focus. Working with others will help ensure you are able to fully research, discuss and better understand the technological, political, socio-economic and/or cultural factors. Looking at how they may have influenced the production of the piece by giving you a chance to conduct more thorough research and by giving you a forum to discuss the group findings.

Once you have identified the pieces of work you want to focus on for the vocational assessment you could use the group as a 'sounding board' for your ideas and theories. This would form part of your individual responsibilities in the second part of the WWO work. All individuals would be expected to be active participants both in terms of presenting and sharing ideas with the group, and with regard to encouraging and reassuring other group participants. These could form the basis of some of the group's individual and collective targets.

Early group work would be based around establishing:

- How, where and when to meet
- How to take decisions
- Timelines (some of which will be determined by the deadlines set by your vocational course)
- Where to look for information
- Who will do what
- How you will work together

The WWO work is focused on the collection of information and discussion; you will be expected to give an individual response to the vocational course requirements. However, you may find the WWO activity useful in practising how to talk about the artistic influences that have affected the style, content and presentation of pieces. You may also be better prepared to show a coherent interpretation of the effects of technological change, socio-economic and cultural factors and be confident about giving a personal response to your selected pieces, having used the group as a way to test and rehearse ideas.

Opportunities

Performing work

This type of topic probably represents one of your best chances to generate course and key skill work simultaneously. As you begin to organise your group look closely at the course requirements and the WWO evidence requirements, identifying where overlap exists and where there may be differences. You may find that the WWO requirements break down what you need to do when working with others into more detail. By meeting the WWO requirements you may well be automatically generating appropriate evidence for your vocational course requirements. Production diaries are useful as evidence for WWO as well. Make sure you evaluate your own performance, reflect on group work and keep track of your individual responsibilities and deadlines in your diary. All this will be useful in your WWO work.

Creating work for performance

This type of activity represents another good opportunity to generate WWO evidence as you work on the vocational requirements. You should be able to use the objectives that come from planning a piece for performance as your WWO objectives as well. The roles and responsibilities, targets and deadlines, planning and team organisation should all be the same.

Make sure you spend time as a team looking at both sets of evidence requirements (WWO and creating work for a performance) and discuss where the overlaps and differences are between the two. Do this before you start any vocational work because the relationship between the two activities is quite extensive and begins right at the early stages as you discuss and plan how to create the piece.

Improving own learning and performance

Skill development

Your Performing Arts course may have a unit that focuses on skill development, getting you to produce a working notebook, which shows how your skills have developed. If so, this is probably your best and easiest way to generate LP evidence while you try to meet the Performing Arts requirements.

You need to spend time identifying where the overlaps between the two sets of evidence requirements are and be aware of where there are any differences. Generally speaking, your notebook and any video recording and audio work focusing on your skills learning and development for your Performing Arts portfolio can also be used in your LP portfolio.

Choosing an area of interest

You may want to specialise or progress into a particular field within the performing arts and entertainment industry. If so, the LP can help you devise a learning programme (targets + plan) to help you pursue your particular interest further while generating evidence for your key skill portfolio at the same time. Perhaps the course deals with your chosen area only briefly. Your LP work can help you investigate the area more thoroughly, looking into the area in more detail.

The aim is not to try to replace or cut across your course work or class learning but support it by developing a learning strategy that complements the work. You can help ensure that your LP work extends or builds on your course work in an appropriate way by involving your teachers in the target-setting process and by using them as a source of feedback. Because your LP work is about learning and improving and centres on your Performing Arts work, your course teachers are appropriate people to offer support and can advise you on how to create and implement your learning plan.

Your chosen area of interest could be anything from:

- A specific type of performance art
- A particular historical period
- Different productions of the same piece
- Something more technical relating to staging a production

The topic could be a particular interest you have either as a hobby or perhaps it is a career aspiration. Your chosen focus could even be a section of the course that features in a higher level course you may want to move on to after this one, in which case you may want to give yourself a good, extensive grounding in the area. Alternatively, it may be something that you struggle with on the course and your aim is to develop an independent learning programme to help you cope with the problem area and develop more confidence in dealing with it in any course work or external assessment you may have to do.

In developing your programme, you need to consider:

- What resources are available to help you
- A suitable time frame for improving your learning and performance
- How you can tell if you are improving
- When you should review your progress

Problem solving

Creating work for performance

Rather than using the process of creating a performance piece as an opportunity to generate WWO evidence, you could use it as a PS opportunity. You could do both, but beware of taking on too much as you juggle work for two key skills as well as your vocational work.

Make sure you are fully aware of what is involved in meeting the PS requirements and spend some time mapping out where an overlap between PS and your vocational work exists. That way you will know what evidence can be used for both courses. The PS work will probably focus more on the logistics of creating a piece for performance. This topic could be a part of a wider PS activity, which includes staging the performance piece. Discuss your intentions with your Performing Arts teacher and key skills tutor before going too far with your plans and targets.

COURSE-RELATED OPPORTUNITIES | **171**

Performing work

Much of the guidance and advice given above in relation to creating a piece for performance applies here also, especially the part about being careful to not take on too much if you are considering WWO work as well. Make sure you are fully aware of the PS key skill requirements before you start because there will be particular types of activity issues and evidence you need to address that may not feature in the vocational course.

Retail and Distributive Services

See also: **Business**, on page 115, and **Travel and Tourism**, on page 179, for further ideas

Context

You will find opportunities for each of the key skills throughout your Retail and Distributive Services (RDS) course. Start early on in the course by identifying where the best opportunities exist. Ideally you want to try to generate evidence for both the key skill and your vocational course simultaneously. This will help cut down on the amount of extra work you need to do to gain the key skill. Look carefully at the vocational course context and the key skill requirements and identify where any overlap in demands exists or where the two different sets of requirements have compatible or related activities.

Working with others

Marketing

Any large-scale marketing activity you need to do – for example, creating and implementing a marketing plan for a retail or distributive service organisation – represents a good opportunity to generate WWO evidence. This may be best done in small groups with the WWO emphasis on collecting primary and secondary data and analysing the findings, as well as discussing ideas for promotional plans. This way you are able to interpret and act on the data you collect individually. You could also use the WWO team to discuss any SWOT and PEST work you need to carry out using them as a forum to sound out ideas and findings.

Working in a team to conduct primary and secondary research may be beneficial. As a result of working in a team you will be able to:

- Brainstorm with team members and discuss the most appropriate ways to collect data
- Employ a range of primary methods or be able to apply one method more widely
- Use the group as a forum to evaluate the effectiveness and suitability of your chosen methods
- Discuss findings and possible conclusions

Your WWO plan and target timelines will relate to:

- Deciding how you will collect your data (working arrangements)
- When and where you will collect data
- Who will do what (roles and responsibilities)
- What you will do with the information when you have collected it

Remember that the RDS course is concerned with the data you collect and how you use it in a marketing capacity, whereas WWO is all about working in a group effectively. Though the two sets of demands are complementary, the evidence you need to create for both will be different.

Developments in retail and distributive services

Consider using this type of topic as an opportunity to generate evidence for WWO. Focus attention on collecting the necessary information and material needed to meet the vocational requirements. For example, if you are asked to illustrate trends in retail and distributive services the WWO work could focus on gathering information on consumer behaviour and shopping patterns, changes in employment patterns, technology and other economic factors and the role of legislation. As a group you will have to agree:

- What is appropriate information
- Where it might be found
- How you need to organise it

Over and above this, the group needs to discuss the deadlines for collecting the information and create a plan of action.

The group can also become a useful forum to discuss how the information collected applies in a local context and can discuss potential local examples drawn from your local high street, shopping centres or shopping mall. You can also look at differences between local data and trends and the national picture.

At this point the nature of WWO would change, with the group no longer concerned with collecting information but instead focusing on how to use and apply it in a local context. This will need to be reflected in your planning, timelines and objectives and means that the expectations change for particular individuals. Individual roles and responsibilities are no longer about the timely collection of useful information, but relate more to active participation in group analysis of the information. The change in remit (from collection of information to discussion of findings) also gives you an opportunity to review group performance and effectiveness, meeting another part of the evidence requirements of the key skill.

Remember that while retail courses will be concerned with the quality of information you collect and what you do with it, WWO is more concerned with how you:

- Work with others
- Participate in the work of the group

- Contribute to the effectiveness of the group
- Collaborate and co-operate with the group members
- Carry out your individual and collective responsibilities

Improving own learning and performance

Finance and retail and distributive services

Finance is an area that has caused students concern in the past. If you think you may find it difficult why not make it the focus of an LP key skill activity. Your aim would be to devise a learning programme to support your course work, giving you more practice in certain areas and helping you to learn about the area independently and at your own pace.

If you can narrow down your focus, try targeting specific areas like budgeting, forecasting and costing or balance sheets and profit and loss accounting rather than having one large general goal. This will help you tackle the problems by focusing your efforts on the exact areas you think may cause you difficulty.

Quality assurance and customer care

Quality assurance may well be a new subject to you. Though it seldom appears in courses, it is a very important concept that tends to increase in importance and relevance the further you study or train. With this in mind it may be worth singling out quality assurance as a topic well worth reinforcing and learning more about. By using the key skill, and making quality assurance the focus of your LP activity, you can increase your confidence in the area and better prepare for any assessments you may have to do. This will be especially helpful if this type of topic is externally assessed.

The object is to use LP to support, complement and extend your class work, not replace it. With this in mind, discuss your intentions with your vocational leader and key skills tutor and agree appropriate targets and timelines for your learning programme. Start to work on the target-setting process, establishing timelines and identifying who could be useful sources of support and guidance. You also need to assess what self-help sources are available. Are there any 'teach yourself' books, revision guides, specialist CD-ROMs and/or specimen exam papers that can be used?

Another important aspect of the planning will be to identify the opportunities to monitor your progress. You need to identify opportunities to use the learning and skills you are developing and get feedback on your progress. This means identifying course work occasions and internal tests or exams where you can see how much you are improving and get feedback on your progress.

Problem solving

Marketing

The creation of an effective marketing plan for a retail or distributive service organisation can be presented in a problem-solving context. Any primary or secondary research you are required to do feeds into the process and represents an attempt to find out more about solving the problem and coming up with an appropriate solution.

Any SWOT or PEST work also feeds into this process and the creation of a promotional plan resulting from your research would represent the potential solution (for the purpose of the key skill).

Merchandising

In a similar vein to marketing, merchandising could be set in a problem-solving context. The production of an informed, well-presented and effective merchandising and display strategy would then be seen as the solution to how to merchandise and display the product or service.

You could start with an analysis of the merchandising technique used and build from there. This type of approach encourages you to apply your vocational knowledge, skills and understanding and allows you to use much of the evidence you create for the 'Problem solving' key skill in your vocational course (and vice versa).

Science

Context

The following suggestions are for courses like A-level Physics, Chemistry and Biology as well as the Vocational A-level in Science and science-related courses. The suggestions focus on generic types of activities that should feature in a range of different courses. You may find that a particular specialist course, e.g. Biology or Physics, and particular syllabuses favour opportunities to generate evidence for one key skill more than another. To fully appreciate what opportunities exist within your own course, find out what types of activities you will be doing and how you will be assessed.

Working with others

The buddy system

There might be aspects of your investigation work or projects that you can do either with a work partner or in small groups. There may even be a range of different experiments that you will be performing across a range of different course topics or units throughout your Science course. If so, consider working with a lab partner for the duration.

Working with a lab partner will help provide you with a substantial example of working on a one-to-one basis. You need to show you can negotiate and agree roles and responsibilities and that you are capable of working together effectively to complete your scientific work successfully. Keep records of your lab work together in a suitable journal and discuss your progress together.

Wider-scale investigations of experimental work may allow you to work in smaller groups generating further WWO evidence.

Improving own learning and performance

Preparing for examinations

Your focus could be on the practical elements of your examination or on the written papers. Basically you would be using the LP key skill as a way of identifying what will be expected of you in either aspect of the exam and establishing a series of targets and a plan to help you prepare. It would focus not so much on the content, but more on the examination techniques that you need to develop in order to make effective use of the time available to get across what you know and understand and the skills that you have.

You need to spend time with your teacher to find out the types of techniques, discipline and skills that will need to be developed. Then you need to develop a plan that targets these areas. You need a learning programme to follow and opportunities to practise and rehearse your performance. Then you will need to find ways to get feedback on how well you did and to provide you with pointers to help you improve further.

Working on experimental and investigative skills

You may be required to develop and plan an experimental and investigative activity. This could be tied to a course work assessment that will count towards your final grade or might be tied into an aspect of the course learning requirements. Either way you will find that the LP key skill can help you focus your work and provide you with a way to organise your work in a clear and coherent manner. This will be especially important if the course work is part of the final assessment because you could be expected to work independently.

If you tie in your LP targets with the experimental and investigation targets you will be able to generate the evidence simultaneously. The key skill will also help you to think more carefully about your planning, to monitor your work and progress and evaluate your results and work method. These aspects could very well be factors assessed in the course work as well. Try to find out as much as possible about how the course project work will be assessed and see how you can tie these expectations into your LP planning and learning programme.

You may find that the LP key skill gets you into a frame of mind that makes you think more carefully about the science activity, questioning your approach and making you plan more effectively. This may help improve the quality of your work.

Developing a specialist interest

There may be an area of the course that you are particularly interested in and want to explore further. If so, the LP key skill can help provide you with a methodology to help you channel this interest as a learning programme, encouraging you to take responsibility for your learning. The topic could be an area that you think you would like to learn more about because you are interested in it or because you think it will feature in an examination.

Whatever the reason, the LP can help you develop this interest and as you learn more about your chosen subject you will also be generating the evidence you need for the key skill. If you are struggling to think of how to structure your learning targets, discuss them with your teacher. Look for help or inspiration in the information you may have available. For example, there may be a unit or module that has some useful suggestions or criteria that you could use in your own learning programme.

The Vocational A-level, for example, has a range of optional units that may well cover aspects of the area you are interested in. It may also include examples of the type of evidence that would show that you were successful in your learning.

This suggestion is really about improving your performance by carrying out further study involving independent learning.

Progressing on to your next course

If you intend to progress to a more specialist science-related course either at HND or degree level consider using the LP key skill as a way of improving your knowledge, skills and understanding of a topic that will be important in your future course. For example, you may want to specialise in Chemistry or Biology in your next course. Perhaps you have done a little amount in your current course and you think you might want to learn more about it and potentially specialise in it.

This type of approach benefits you by not only preparing you thoroughly for an important topic in your next course, but also by helping you improve your chances of higher grades within your current Science course. You also get to focus your LP work on an area that obviously interests you.

Your LP aim is to extend the learning that takes place in the classroom by getting you to develop a 'learning and skills development programme' that takes you further or deeper into the subject than perhaps your existing course requires. Make sure you discuss with your Science teacher how you can set feasible targets that support, supplement and extend your course work allowing you to explore your particular interest further. Having agreed appropriate targets you can set about devising a programme, making sure you work to an appropriate time frame and have ways both to measure how effectively you are learning and improving your abilities in the area, and to review your progress at sensible points.

You will need to find some way to get feedback and support as well as identifying all the support and self-help materials that may be out there. This includes CD-ROMs and the Internet, which has a number of interesting specialist websites. You also need to spend time identifying an area that you are particularly interested in or will be important later. This will involve carrying out a little research into the type of content covered in the course you want to move on to. You are not aiming to meet the standard in your next course, you are trying to become more familiar with the content. The goal is to make sure you have a solid grounding in the chosen area, and in that way transition on to the higher course will be a little smoother and potentially easier to cope with.

COURSE-RELATED OPPORTUNITIES | **177**

Becoming more confident in a particular topic

Take time to look at the range and type of learning and content awaiting you in the Science course and try to identify areas that may cause you particular problems or difficulty. You could use the areas of content you identify to become the focus of your LP activity. The idea is to focus on potential problem areas early and for you to design and develop as well as implement a learning and improvement strategy to supplement and support your class work. By doing this, the problem content will be less of a threat in terms of the final assessment or your exams. By targeting an area of potential weakness, you will be improving your chances of higher grades in any assessments you do and helping to improve your confidence and command across the course.

Important in this type of approach is:

- Early and thorough exploration of the course content to identify areas of potential concern
- Clear justification to yourself and to others of why the chosen area needs special attention. For example, has it caused problems in a previous course or is it completely new to you?
- Discussion of your plans with both your Science teacher and key skills tutor

You can then start to work on the target-setting process, establishing timelines and identifying who could be useful sources of support and guidance. You also need to assess what self-help sources are available. Are there any 'teach yourself' books, revision guides, specialist CD-ROMs and/or specimen exam papers that can be used?

Another important aspect of the planning will be to identify the opportunities to monitor your progress. You need to identify opportunities to use the learning and skills you are developing and get feedback on your progress. This means identifying course work occasions and internal tests or exams where you can see how much you are improving and get feedback on your progress. Make sure you have a regular dialogue about your progress with your Science teacher to ensure that your learning remains focused on the course syllabus content and you don't wander off into other areas that may add to any confusion.

Don't be too ambitious and pick too large a topic. Try to pick something that will be of real benefit to you. Perhaps you could focus on something that will help improve your understanding significantly, perhaps because it relates to a number of other areas. Hopefully the end result will not only be a suitable portfolio of LP evidence but improved performance in an important area of the course.

Problem solving

In a sense any experimental work, applied and investigative work in science is a type of problem solving. The issue will be whether or not you have a substantial enough science activity to allow you to address the PS requirements in a meaningful way. Discuss with your Science teacher how you could use different topics to help generate PS evidence. There may be certain topics that could be presented as problem-solving case studies that involve investigative methods and experiments to help solve.

Areas to consider to could include:

- Controlling fluid flow
- Managing energy
- Increasing the useful energy transfer to improve efficiency, or detecting useful and wasteful energy transfers in a system
- Diagnosis techniques
- Working out ecological relationships
- Establishing and explaining properties of materials

Look in particular at the type of internal assessment you will be required to do as part of your course. Many syllabuses have a significant amount of internal assessment in the form of projects or investigations. This might be your opportunity to meet the PS requirements as well as do your science work at the same time.

Travel and Tourism

See also: **Business**, page 115, **Leisure and Recreation**, page 154, and **Retail and Distributive Services**, page 172, for further ideas

Context

Travel and Tourism courses cover a range of different core subjects and will include opportunities to specialise in areas of particular interests. Take time to get a clear picture of the range of different subjects that you cover and find out a little about each. Then you can look at which units give you the best opportunities to generate key skill evidence. Once you have looked at the suggestions below, you should also look at the guidance in courses related to Travel and Tourism, like Business and Leisure and Recreation.

Working with others

Marketing

If the emphasis in your marketing course or unit is on actually creating marketing strategies and carrying out market research consider using this as an opportunity for generating WWO evidence. Look at the advice given in the Business courses guide, page 115.

Travel and tourism in action

At some point in your Travel and Tourism course you will get a chance to plan an event or to carry out a team project. Look for opportunities to work in a group to produce and implement a business plan for either the event or project. These can be turned into your WWO objectives as well. For WWO your intended outcomes would be a logical and coherent

business plan, a successfully run and executed team project or event and effective working arrangements and relationships. These may also be aspects of the vocational course requirements.

Other areas of overlap that may produce evidence capable of being used in both your vocational course and your WWO portfolio of evidence include:

- Effective planning throughout the project, keeping appropriate records of all team meetings
- Specifying objectives and establishing individual roles and responsibilities
- Consideration of resource needs (physical, human, financial), legal obligations and timescales
- Effective participation in running the project
- Keeping records of your own individual contribution
- Analysis of your own and the team's performance

Look carefully at the overlap and differences in the two sets of evidence requirements (Travel and Tourism and WWO) and discuss in your team the work that can be used for both and the extra work that may need to be done for each.

Keep in mind the evidence of your own individual contributions that will need to appear in both portfolios as well as the collectively generated evidence. You also have a chance to meet the WWO requirements as an effective, supportive and considerate team player to begin to meet some of the vocational higher grade requirements. Identify the possibilities for meeting the higher vocational grades early and factor these into your own personal WWO plans and objectives.

WWO can help to provide a useful framework for holding your vocational teamwork together. This probably represents your best opportunity in Travel and Tourism to generate WWO evidence without having to do too much additional work. Just be careful about subtle differences in the two sets of evidence requirements. In fact this could be a topic for discussion at an early group meeting.

Keep talking to both your Travel and Tourism teacher and your WWO assessor to make sure you are on the right tracks with both sets of work.

Improving own learning and performance

Marketing

If the course aims to help you develop an understanding of how UK travel and tourism uses marketing then you may find that you can use this as an LP focus. Don't choose to focus on marketing generally as a target, focus on something a little more specific. Consider a narrower topic like the marketing mix, and think about using the following suggestions to help you frame your targets:

- Understanding the marketing mix and the technical terms associated with it

- The strengths and weaknesses of marketing mixes
- The relationship between marketing mix and market research

Look carefully at the vocational evidence requirements and try to create a coherent set of LP targets around a key part of the course. You may want to focus on reinforcing the learning contained in your marketing course or extend your knowledge of an aspect of the course with some additional learning of your own. Read the guidance that follows for further information.

Supporting your course work or pursuing an area of interest

You can reinforce your course work and the related learning by creating personalised learning targets and goals. These can then be developed into your own learning programme that will help you improve in the course and help you meet the LP requirements. If the aim is to extend your knowledge and understanding then work with your teacher to establish some more ambitious targets that allow you to get deeper into a subject than perhaps the course allows. Either approach will suit the LP key skill.

By really getting to grips with a challenging area of content you can build confidence and be better prepared for any assessment you may have to do. You can use the LP key skill to devise a personal learning programme, setting targets to help you improve your performance in a specific area of the course. The aim is to support your normal course and class work, not replace it, so consult your teacher and get advice on how to set appropriate targets and feasible goals.

Alternatively, if you are coping well with the course demands, why not use the LP key skill to develop a learning programme that could extend your knowledge, skills and understanding in a specific area of Travel and Tourism? By digging deeper into a specific area or interest you may either cover some useful groundwork for a higher course you intend to do, or you may improve your chances to get higher grades in your current course.

If you know the course you want to take next (i.e. an HND, or even degree) consider looking at the types of content that will feature heavily in the first term or year of the course and choose an aspect of it you wish to find out more about. You are not trying to meet the higher standards of the course through your LP work; rather, you are devising a learning programme based on doing some background preparation, making sure you have a good grounding in the content area. This may make the transition on to the course a little smoother. If you don't want to take this type of approach then just choose a topic within your current course that you are particularly interested in and want to pursue further on your own. Your course teachers should be able to offer help and advice.

You need to consider what additional resources you can use. There may be self-help books, CD-ROMs or websites that you can use. You also need to find ways to monitor and review your progress. Make sure your Travel and Tourism teacher and your LP assessor are happy with your targets and your extra work.

Problem solving

Marketing

The whole issue of determining how effectively businesses use marketing could be set in a PS context. Working out how successful or effective a marketing strategy is for a company could be an exercise in detection, investigation and research.

SWOT and PEST analyses could become activities to help you find out more about marketing and business and could be used in both your vocational course and your WWO portfolio of evidence. You could either look at a particular type of marketing in general, for example the effectiveness of the Internet as an advertising agent, or look at the strategy of one company in particular, producing an appraisal of the company's marketing strategy. The PS key skill could help you by providing a useful methodology and framework to help you focus your efforts. This type of activity could also be a useful way of reinforcing your vocational learning and could be a good way of preparing you for an external assessment involving marketing.

Evidence from other activities

Creating a webpage

Context

Creating a webpage has the potential to be the focus of not just a WWO key skill activity but also LP and PS activities. Though this signpost takes you through the steps related to WWO, many of the questions and issues addressed will be the same if you go down the LP or PS route.

Within WWO, creating a webpage could be carried out for a 'client' (i.e. working to a brief) or with a partner. It could also be done as the focus of group work.

The signpost indicates areas that you will need to address in your WWO activity. However, it doesn't give too much of the 'how to' detail when it comes to actually constructing your webpage. This is because there are a number of options, choices of methods, techniques and resources available to you. Finding out what you need to know and do, evaluating it, and making informed choices, are all part of the WWO activity and will generate appropriate key skill evidence.

The design and creation of a working webpage will be time consuming so you should be able to satisfy the key skill requirements to work over an extended period. It is also a substantial and complex enough task to generate evidence for all aspects of the key skill.

> **WWO** = Working with others
> **LP** = Improving own learning and performance
> **PS** = Problem solving

Plan complex work with others, agreeing objectives, responsibilities and working arrangements

As a group, you are going to have to agree on the purpose and content of your webpage. You need to establish the main objectives and spend a little time carrying out some research into how you will create the webpage. Gathering this information will allow you to set more precise objectives, set targets and agree working arrangements. For example, once you have agreed a purpose you are going to have to consider:

- How to get your page on to the Internet. Which Internet Service Provider will host your site?
- What software are you going to use? Consider the software not just to create your webpage but also for the graphics you might use
- What are the training or learning needs of the group? People will need to learn how to use the software effectively

Opportunities

- What resources, support and guidance are available?
- Are there any financial considerations?

There are a number of ways to create and place webpages on the Internet. You need to establish which methods are the most appropriate to you. The choices will range from simple 'one-stop shop' approaches where you use a single integrated software package to do everything, to more sophisticated methods using a number of different software products. You need to establish what software is available to you, establish its potential and learn how to use it effectively.

Useful places to find guidance include:

- Self-help manuals; for example, there are a number of 'How to' guides for beginners that deal with designing and creating your own webpages
- Software manuals; for example, companies producing the software also have manuals to show you how to use it effectively. Microsoft produces a manual to support its Microsoft Word software. Word has a facility to help you create simple webpages
- The ICT departments in your school, college or workplace

You need to divide up responsibilities based on group members' interests and sort out how you will discuss and monitor progress and take decisions. Everyone should be included in acquiring the knowledge, skills and understanding associated with creating a webpage.

Resist the temptation to keep IT knowledge and learning restricted to a few people. For example, even though there might be one or two who are already very familiar with the task or a particular software application, everyone should be involved. Be careful not to let the more confident people take over the design and creation aspects leaving others just to write content. You can avoid this problem by working in a group with people who have a similar level of familiarity with computers and the Internet. This way the more knowledgeable or experienced people can work on a more advanced project and less experienced people can get involved in a more straightforward webpage.

Try to encourage everyone to develop a basic familiarity with the technical language and relevant processes involved in creating a webpage. Set this as a target for the group. You may wonder how you could assess whether you have met the target successfully. One indicator would be whole group involvement in the more technical discussions and decision taking and everyone's developing an understanding of the technical language and showing that they are comfortable using it. In later meetings of the group, you could ask a teacher or assessor to sit in and witness everyone's active participation in discussions of technical detail, or alternatively the teacher or assessor could ask technical questions of group members. Progress in terms of the learning and development of team members might be more evident if the teacher or assessor is invited to sit in on an early meeting where people are just beginning the learning process.

If you intend to use this type of approach, you need to explain to the observer why you want them to sit in on the meetings.

Seek to establish and maintain co-operative relationships over an extended period of time, agreeing changes to achieve agreed targets

There should be an opportunity for group members to share their work with others using different drafts of their work. Perhaps, members with different responsibilities could present their work to the group at a meeting. You may also find that, depending on how you have divided up the task, some members' progress is dependent on the work of others. So careful planning, monitoring and communication will be very important.

All this means that you will need to establish how you can set up a regular forum for reporting progress and taking decisions. This will also provide you with a means to generate evidence for this aspect of the key skill.

Individually, you need to be clear about your role, who you will work closely with and precisely what your timelines are. Ask yourself:

- What are my individual targets and work responsibilities?
- How do I relay these to others? Who needs to know?
- What training or support do I need?
- Who can help me?
- How can I contribute to group organisation and decision taking?
- Who do I need to work closely with?
- Am I dependent on input from another group member in order to achieve my goals?
- Do I have an influential role on the work of particular group members?
- How to do I monitor my work and report progress to the group?

Review work with others and agree ways of improving collaborative work in the future

There are a few basic ideas to consider when looking to evaluate the WWO activity. The first relates to the final product itself: your webpage. Evaluate how it looks and performs on the Internet, looking at whether or not it does what you wanted it to do.

You could even put an evaluation questionnaire on your webpage explaining the context and asking a few simple feedback questions. This could be a line of development and responsibility for a few individuals in the group. You would need to identify this as a distinct target at the start of the process, making it the responsibility of particular group members. They then need to learn how to create an online evaluation and develop the questionnaire, having it ready to launch along with the webpage.

If this sounds too ambitious, a simple model might be a link on the webpage to an email address, with visitors to the site invited to email their feedback using the link. This means you need to look at how to create a link to an email address and agree what areas you want the feedback to address. You may also need to establish an email account. Alternatively, you could ask individuals to view the webpage and feed back their

Opportunities

opinions. This could be done in a controlled manner by giving them a set questionnaire to answer as they view the page. Alternatively, you could use a less structured format by just asking them to give their own thoughts and impressions based on their visit to the page. You can discuss in your group how you want to do this, setting appropriate targets and timelines.

Other evaluation considerations include:

- How did you do in terms of your timelines?
- Did you work to budget?
- What else influenced the outcome?

How the group worked together is the other focus for your evaluation. Try to reach agreement on the lessons learned and how you could improve. One way to look at the group performance is to discuss how much more the group has learned about how to create a webpage. For example, do individual members now feel confident enough to create a page themselves. This is a general account of the 'up-skilling' that has gone on in the group. Indirectly, it also gives you an indication of who may have been left out or left behind in the general group work. Look at:

- How well did you meet your objectives?
- How effective was the way you took decisions?
- How helpful were the resources and support materials?
- Was the 'progress monitoring' effective?
- Was the strategy for communication and reporting effective?

Producing a publication

Context

Publications involve a lot of hard work and dedication. Don't start one just to do the key skill. Get involved because it is something you want to do and then use the key skill as a way to help you organise your efforts.

Producing a regular magazine, newsletter or similar publication is a useful way of generating evidence for this key skill. The production of a publication that is interesting, marketable and popular is a challenge that many have tried. The 'Working with others' key skill provides a framework that can help you create and maintain a publication, making it an important part of the school, college or workplace.

Publishing requires the successful combination of a range of skills and talents and continued success can only really be achieved by establishing an effective team. Specific roles, tasks and responsibilities can be allocated using the general headings of:

- Editorial
- Production (including generation of copy)
- Distribution
- Marketing and Sales

Successful publication may well be an overall aim but your targets will be much smaller and will relate to all the different aspects of production.

Plan complex work with others, agreeing objectives, responsibilities and working arrangements

Start with the formation of a group of like-minded people keen to take on this type of project. Meet to discuss the type of publication you all want to produce. Things to consider:

- Purpose and target audience
- Frequency
- Content
- Size
- Cost
- Financing
- Title

You also need to decide who does what. Start by thinking about the roles that are required. Think of the three phases of pre-production, production and post-production. Questions that you need to consider include:

- Who will gather information and generate copy?
- Who will edit material and design layout?
- What about liaison with others to secure resources, e.g. printing and supplies of paper?
- Who will take responsibility for distribution?

Think of others that need to be involved. Are there people who control access to the equipment and resources you may need? What about permission? Remember to organise your meetings and keep records.

You don't need to rush into anything. The first few meetings can be about research and fact-finding so you know exactly what is involved. This will help you allocate roles and plan more effectively. Set targets for each meeting that means each person has a task to do for the next meeting. You may even have to do some market research to establish the kind of publication people would like to see available. This would introduce a set of targets and tasks before you even start producing your publication. However, it will help you find out what people would be prepared to read and may save a lot of wasted effort.

Think carefully about doing market research and dismiss it at your peril. Once you have the results of your research you will know much more about what a publication will have to do if it is to be successful.

Also take time to find out what advice or help is available. There could be helpful 'starter packs' available either in pamphlet or book form or on the Internet. There could be support groups or agencies that produce 'support packs' for setting up newspapers, etc. Start by finding out what support materials are available. Think about who might be a source of useful information in your school, college or community (for example, in a local library of even local newspaper).

Seek to establish and maintain co-operative working relationships over an extended period of time, agreeing changes to achieve agreed objectives

Once you are up and running, you need to synchronise your personal targets and responsibilities with those of the team and the publication cycle. Depending on the regularity of your publication, try to include at least two editions as the time frame for your key skill evidence. This should be sufficient to meet the 'extended period of time' key skill requirement and will also show that you are able to create and maintain co-operative working relationships. The production of one edition might be sufficient as a time frame for the key skill if you also include the teamwork involved in doing the market research. Check with your teacher or assessor to establish what would be a suitable time frame.

Review work with others and agree ways of improving collaborative work in the future

At each stage of the production cycle take stock as a group. Look at where you are at and how you got there, recording views on what worked well or proved difficult and what approaches might be worth repeating or are better discarded.

Look at your own performance as an individual and as a group member. You may find that a survey of reader attitudes about the publication provides useful feedback to help you review your work as a group. Reader opinion may prove to be the ultimate gauge of your success. Think carefully about the questions you will ask your readers and try to frame them in a way that will provide you with pointers for how to get better. This can be hard to do with just 'Yes' or 'No' questions.

Running a club or event

Context

In most schools, colleges or workplaces there will be opportunities to work with others by running a club, society or organising an event. This could be anything from a school chess club, work social evening or picnic, college disco or even trade union related work. You could be setting something up, or taking over the organisation and running it for a while, so your WWO could be done by using an ongoing activity. Alternatively, it could be a one-off event, with WWO covering the initial planning, organisation and running of the event.

Plan complex work with others, agreeing objectives, responsibilities and working arrangements

Your objectives will really depend on the type of activity you intend to use for WWO. However, most activities will involve some or most of the following:

- Venue
- Dates
- Health and safety
- Access to equipment or other resources
- Costs
- Scheduling
- Communication

Communication could involve advertising for one-off events or starting, maintaining or improving the communication necessary to run a club or society. The factors listed above, do not deal with the actual 'content', i.e. what will happen on the day of the event or during the club or meeting. You will need objectives to cover these as well.

If you look at the list above you will see that responsibility for each may lie with different people. Therefore you may have a range of people to liaise with to get what you need done.

You need to agree individual responsibilities and working arrangements within the group. If you are using participation in an existing club or society as the focus of your WWO there may already be established divisions of labour. For example, there may be a chairperson, secretary, treasurer, etc.

By the end of the first stage of the WWO activity you all need to agree:

- What it is you are using as the focus for WWO
- Who will do what
- What the working arrangements are

The types of issues to consider when agreeing working arrangements include:

- How decisions will be taken
- How you will communicate with each other
- What time considerations need to be addressed

Note that in ongoing activities, like running a club, it will be useful to give yourself and the group some sort of end-date or target to work towards. This way you can review how things have gone once you have reached this point, even if the work needs to continue. Try to identify a major event, e.g. an annual general meeting, the last meeting of term, and use this as your end-target.

Your objectives can start and stop and new ones can be set that run past the end-date or end-target. You will be using the end-date for your WWO as a way of reviewing your progress, discussing how you met objectives and reviewing where you are with regard to ongoing work.

Seek to establish and maintain co-operative relationships over an extended period of time, agreeing changes to achieve agreed targets

This is where you get on with business, whether it is running a club or preparing for a one-off event. As you organise the work keep evidence that shows you are co-operating with others in your group and are communicating progress where appropriate. Meetings (and the paperwork that goes with them) are useful sources of evidence for your WWO portfolio. For example, minutes can be a useful record of the decisions that have been taken and by having someone (an assessor or teacher) sit in on the meeting you will have a written testament of your participation in the meeting.

In meetings you should not only play your part in the decision-making process but encourage others to do so as well.

Meetings can be useful venues to renegotiate objectives and agree changes to working arrangements. They are also useful forums for exchanging information and reporting on your individual progress. Journals or diaries are also useful records of your individual planning, thoughts and work on your contribution to the group work.

Review work with others and agree ways of improving collaborative work in the future

You need to review the group performance at some point. There will be sensible dates, for example either directly after the event you've organised or at the end of term or after an important meeting like an AGM, to carry out the review, so try to identify when this will be and plan for it.

Your review will need to address:

- The extent to which working with others has been successful
- How you did in terms of meeting your objectives
- Factors that have influenced the outcome
- Ways of improving WWO in future

In ongoing work you can act on the ways you think you can improve your WWO.

Journals can be a useful way to record your own thoughts of how you are doing in terms of carrying out your responsibilities as well as being a way to record your thoughts on the group work. This way you have a record of your thoughts on work and the progress made at the time and you won't need to try to do all this at the end. Effective reviewing should be an ongoing process that shouldn't just be left until the end of the WWO activity. Every time you meet with others, you will have an opportunity to review and discuss the work to date and have a chance to make any necessary adjustments.

Study groups

Context

One interesting way of collecting evidence for WWO is to organise a study group. If you have important examinations to study for (e.g. A-level) or will be doing some extensive coursework (e.g. a Vocational A-level project or course work for A-level) then consider using the WWO key skill to help you organise your efforts more effectively. You will benefit in two ways:

- Potentially improving your course grades
- Generating evidence for your key skill

There are two key points to remember to help make the experience a success. Firstly, find a small number of like-minded people who are motivated and want to do well in the work that you decide to use as your WWO focus. This will make it a more rewarding experience. Secondly, in this instance, though the key skill is important, it should take on a supporting role to help you perform better in your examination or do well in your course work. The deadlines for your target work will probably be less flexible than for your WWO.

This is a good way to generate evidence because it gets you to think about taking greater responsibility and control over your own learning and progress. The earlier you get started and the more time you give yourself, the better you will be.

This doesn't necessarily have to be a group activity. You could focus on the one-to-one requirements and find yourself a 'study buddy' rather than a study group. If this is how you prefer to do it, the advice below is still the same.

Plan complex work with others, agreeing objectives, responsibilities and working arrangements

As a study group you need to:

- Be clear about the group focus
- Discuss what the group will actually do, e.g. discuss particular topics, focus on discussing key questions or assignments, review and discuss that week's or month's learning

You must be clear on the discussion of homework questions and course work that may carry marks. The study group is not about all working together to do the work, it is about helping each other become more aware of the issues, topics and concepts involved. It is about preparing each other to be able to then go and meet the challenges set as individuals. At the end of the day, you will all be graded either in an examination or by your teacher as individuals, so use WWO to support each other while learning about the subject and keep this distinct from your individual performance in any assessments.

Opportunities

- Set your goal as something feasible and measurable. Don't go for something like 'Do better in the exam' or 'Get a better grade'. Discuss in your group what key aspect of a course you could focus on, consider the issues that are involved and generate a more precise set of objectives for yourselves
- Set small-scale targets that can be built upon. This will only be possible if you devote plenty of time to organisation. As you reach each target or milestone review your progress. Milestones could be built around homework deadlines, mock exams, mid-term or end-of-term breaks. All of these give you a chance to review your progress as a group
- Discuss how you will manage the different timelines for your primary goal (the course you are taking) and the supporting goal (WWO)
- Share with the group what each member wants out of the experience and what your own individual targets need to be
- Remember to keep a record of discussions and decision taking to use as evidence for your key skill portfolio. Discuss and record how the group's activities can support individual and team objectives
- Establish how, when and where you will meet and what you will discuss and study. Will you each prepare something and bring it to discuss? Will you take turns? How will you decide what should happen from one meeting to the next? (Keep creating and filing the evidence for your key skill but keep in mind the real focus is on your primary work so leave plenty time and space for getting on with that)
- Try to allocate about 15–20% of the time to the WWO progress and organisation, focusing particularly on the study group work. Use the key skill to facilitate the running and management of the group

Seek to establish and maintain co-operative relationships over an extended period of time, agreeing changes to achieve agreed targets

Getting started is often the easiest part. Keeping your group focus, momentum and motivation is often harder. Be prepared to make changes to help keep the group effective.

Keep reviewing the frequency of study group meetings and the venue. Only time will tell if you are meeting too often or too infrequently. Both can have their problems. For example, too often may mean that you don't have enough to discuss, attendance by everyone isn't always possible or it becomes a chore. Meeting too infrequently could mean that you forget what to do, begin to lack motivation or feel embarrassed discussing something in front of others.

Keep evaluating your venue, ask yourselves:

- Are there too many distractions?
- Is it inconvenient for some members?

As you monitor your study group progress, judge its effectiveness by how better or more confident you feel about the subject you focus on. This is the real measure of its success.

Review work with others and agree ways of improving collaborative work in the future

Bring in outside help to give you an objective opinion on your collective and individual progress. If you choose a school or college library to work in, see if an appropriate teacher can join one of your sessions.

Does any homework you do show signs that you are improving? Are class test results getting better? These are all things that can provide your group with important feedback on your collective and individual progress.

Work out what is going well and what is going less well. Especially look at your in-group relationships and how you are doing individually and collectively in the chosen subject as a result of the group. Review your work after each major piece of subject work you do or at convenient breaks like half-term or end of term. Try to identify factors that are helping or hindering the study group and how you could all overcome these. Are you meeting your original objectives? How can you improve?

Once you have decided on a strategy to improve collaborative work in future, celebrate it by putting it into effect with the launch of 'Study Group II'.

Homework and course work strategies

Context

This isn't about making a single piece of homework or course work become the focus of your key skill evidence. It is about considering the range of homework or course work that will need to be done during the course of your studies. This will mean that you need to devise a learning and improvement strategy that will last for a significant length of time. This should be a sustained effort. Think of it as a one-term minimum effort depending on the amount of homework or course work you need to do.

The key skill can help you devise an appropriate methodology to help organise your efforts, and as you improve your homework or course work, you will also be collecting evidence along the way for your LP key skill. So this type of approach benefits your course performance and as you improve you also generate evidence for your LP portfolio.

Agree targets and plan how these will be met over an extended period of time, using support from appropriate people

Start by asking your teacher/tutor to comment on the content and style of

an initial piece of homework or course work and get as much information as possible about it. Think of the information you need under the headings:

- Knowledge and understanding of the topic
- Presentation
- Grammar, punctuation and spelling
- Specialist vocabulary
- Any other observations on your work

These headings can be developed into criteria to help you monitor and evaluate your progress and performance. This lets you know what you are up against in terms of the aspects of your work that can be strengthened. They also give you an opportunity to create clear and realistic targets to enable you to improve your performance. Discuss what you are trying to do with the LP skill with your teacher or teachers.

You could focus on improving your work across two or more courses, it doesn't have to be just one course. The more courses you focus on, the more varied your targets might be, because there will be a range of time-lines and feedback from different people to take into account. There may also be different skills involved in doing well in each of your subjects, so you need to identify these early on and build them into your strategy for improving your performance.

Base your plan around actual coursework deadlines or events. Make sure you also use the full range of resources at your disposal. For example, libraries, self-help guides and teaching staff. Perhaps there are exercises on CD-ROM that can help you improve on certain aspects of your work. The Internet may also offer useful support. Spend time looking at the range of resources both in the school, college or workplace and in the local area that may be available to you.

Take responsibility for your learning by using your plan, and seeking feedback and support from relevant sources, to help meet targets

Any level 3 work, e.g. A-level or Vocational A-level, will be sufficiently complex for the key skill purposes.

Every piece of work you submit for comment, marking or assessment by teaching staff can be treated as an important piece of key skill evidence that charts your progress towards your goals. Treat the return of this work to you as an opportunity to review your progress and reflect on how well you are moving towards meeting your targets and briefly record your thoughts.

Make sure you share with the person marking your work your thoughts on what you are trying to achieve and ask them to give you full feedback on each area you have identified as needing improvement. Discuss any areas of the feedback you are unsure about and ask for further advice or comment on areas of work not commented on.

Review progress on two occasions and establish evidence of achievements, including how you have used learning from other tasks to meet new demands

You will need to review and reflect on your progress every time you get feedback in the form of marking or assessment of work. This way you will be able to see how much progress you are making. Act on this feedback by altering your working methods or plans to adapt to this input. Write up your new targets or alterations in a work journal or diary.

Keep feedback and the marks for your course work or homework assessment as evidence of your progress. Even if the marks are not as good as you had hoped for, they can still form an important part of the portfolio. Combine them with your own notes on why you think you didn't get the marks you hoped for as well as notes on how you altered your LP strategy to try to improve. Any follow-up discussion you have with your teacher should also be kept along with your thoughts on the discussion. You may even find it helpful to read your own work again after you have read the comments on it and discussed them with your teacher. Then you can give an honest appraisal of your work yourself.

It is worth doing this type of evaluation exercise at the end of any piece of work you submit and get back. However, as well as this ongoing evaluation, which will be important to keep you focused, also consider two major review stages. Build in a half-way evaluation of progress and then a final evaluation towards the end of the course. Following a normal school or college year, you could build in a half-way revision at Christmas and then a final one at Easter. Alternatively, if you have enough homework or course work to justify the approach, you could use the half-term and end-of-term breaks as your review stages. Both suggestions certainly give you an extended period of time to establish, implement and reflect on your strategy to improve your homework or course work performance.

Outward bound courses and extra-curricular activities

Context
This signpost aims to give you an indication of how you can use the 'Improving own learning and performance' key skill in other types of courses or challenges you could be taking. The context doesn't really matter too much, you should still be able to generate some LP evidence. Examples of outward bound or extra-curricular courses that could be used, include:

- Duke of Edinburgh awards
- Adventure Scout courses
- Life saving awards

- Survival challenges
- Music grade awards

The LP key skill can provide a useful framework for organising your extra-curricular efforts and help ensure success. As you strive towards these goals, you will generate LP evidence along the way. So it should be a win–win situation.

Agree targets and plan how these will be met over an extended period of time, using support from appropriate people

You should be able to merge the targets that you use to base your LP key skill activity around with the targets in your extra-curricular activity. Timescales should also be compatible. You are going to let the extra-curricular work take the lead and use the LP as a way of supporting you. Try to collapse the targets and plans for the LP into your extra-curricular activity as much as possible. If there are no plans, just a target, then you need to use your LP as a way of developing a suitable and realistic plan of action to achieve your extra-curricular goals. Either way, you need to have considered the following:

- Your targets
- Your plans, including contingency plans
- People who can offer support and guidance
- How you will be assessed in your extra-curricular work

You will basically develop a learning and development programme based around the achievement of extra-curricular goals. This will involve setting review stages of mini-assessments to help you work out what progress you are making and what still needs to be improved. If your activity is more practical based – for example, you may be taking a life saving award or a swimming course – you need to work out a training schedule based on supervised access to the pool. You may need to practise when the pool is quiet, while making sure that you don't interfere with other commitments. In order to make this process effective you need to set targets for practice and training. The same is also true of any of the examples listed above.

You have an obvious list of appropriate people to discuss your LP work with. These include not just your key skills assessor, but also the people involved in your extra-curricular activities. Both will be useful sources of advice when you come to set yourself realistic targets and can help you identify appropriate interim goals and ways to assess your performance.

Take responsibility for your learning by using your plan, and seeking feedback and support from relevant sources, to help meet targets

You need to take the initiative and show you are capable of taking control of and responsibility for your own learning and improvement. However, part of this responsibility includes making sure that you are learning in a safe way, working under appropriate supervision and you must show that you can take account of the appropriate health and safety considerations.

Look to identify an appropriate stage to review your work. Either find a natural break in the learning programme or review your progress after you reach an interim target. Even if your activities are predominantly physical and/or practical, you still need to review your performance and assess how close you are to achieving your targets. This also gives you an opportunity to make adjustments to your plan and/or training schedule, if necessary.

Review progress on two occasions and establish evidence of achievements, including how you have used learning from other tasks to meet new demands

Your final extra-curricular assessment can be used to show your actual achievements. After you have completed the assessment, look back on the whole process and look at the changes you would make to improve your performance in future. This would naturally form the second of the two occasions needed for the LP requirements.

Taking your driving theory test

Context

Learning to drive may be high on your agenda. You must be 17 years old to obtain a provisional licence to drive a motor car. The complete driving test for a motor car has two components: a theory test and a practical test. You need to pass the theory test before you can attempt the driving practical test. The LP key skill could be a useful way to prepare for the theory test and as you learn and improve your knowledge and understanding you will also be generating evidence for your LP portfolio. The LP key skill will help you approach the challenge in a systematic, well-organised way. It will help you think carefully about how to organise your learning and how to monitor your performance.

You can combine both driving practice and preparing for the theory test in your LP work; this would give you the chance to devise a learning and development programme that attempts to improve your performance by studying a complex subject and learning through a complex practical activity. Alternatively, you could target the two aspects of learning to drive separately in two distinct learning and development programmes. This guidance concentrates on devising a plan to address the driving theory test only. The issues you need to address to devise a programme for the practical test will be similar.

The LP work will involve creating a learning programme designed to get you ready to take the theory test. Remember, although the desired end result (a pass in the driving theory test) is important, a record of how you approach the challenge will be necessary for the key skill.

Agree targets and plan how these will be met over an extended period of time, using support from appropriate people

Before you are able to set appropriate targets you need to gather information on how to achieve what you want to do. The types of information you need to collect and the issues you need to address include:

- Completion of documentation to obtain a provisional licence. You must hold a current licence to sit the theory test and can set the necessary administrative process in motion with a visit to the post office to pick up the appropriate form
- Getting acquainted with the procedures and regulations
- Locating your most convenient theory test centre where you can pick up the necessary literature about the test
- Studying the Driving Standards Agency (DSA) leaflet explaining the touch screen computerised theory test
- Checking out the DSA website (**www.driving-tests.co.uk**) which includes the range of publications and products available in book, manual and CD-ROM format
- Investigating the possibility of formal practical driving lessons from an approved instructor so as to enable you to develop practical skills and experience alongside theory acquisition.
- Investigating the costs involved (provisional driving licence; theory test; approved driving lessons instructions; learning resources)

Once you have gathered the necessary information you can begin to think about the kinds of target you will need to set and decide on a realistic time frame. Because you are essentially creating a learning programme for yourself, one of your teachers, e.g. a guidance or subject teacher, may be able to offer you advice on your targets. Alternatively, your driving instructor may be able to offer support and advice.

When devising your learning programme and setting your targets you need to consider:

- How you are going to break up the learning into smaller, more manageable sections and set yourself sensible targets
- When and where you are actually going to study
- Who can help by asking you questions

Take responsibility for your learning by using your plan, and seeking feedback and support from relevant sources, to help meet targets

You now need to implement your planned programme of study. Remember, it is not just a question of memorising information for the test, you are going to have to apply your knowledge and understanding when you come to take the driving test, so if at all possible link your developing theory knowledge with supervised practical experience. Use you instructor fully, discuss what you have learned and find ways to measure your progress. You will need to find out ways to test your knowledge to help you measure how much you have learned and to judge how effective your learning programme is. One way to do this is to take practice theory tests.

You will find practice test questions in various 'teach yourself'-type books and CD-ROMs and you can also take a practice test online using the web address shown above. The Driving Standards Agency has a CD-ROM that contains a question bank and gets you familiar with the type of screen you are likely to see used during the test. This is a useful resource to build into your learning programme.

The online test is a useful way of getting used to the form of questions you might encounter in the actual theory test and will help you get used to using computers to take a test. During the actual driving theory test you select your answers by touching the computer screen. Though you will get a brief practice session to get used to the actual system before starting your theory test, using the online practice tests will give you an early taster of the type of thing to expect. Though there is no time limit when you take the online practice tests, you can begin to introduce time as a factor. It is a factor in the actual test where you are expected to answer 35 questions in 40 minutes. You must get 30 correct answers to pass the actual test. The online test will be automatically marked for you on completion.

Build in a few opportunities to take some form of practice test as a way to monitor your progress.

Review progress on two occasions and establish evidence of achievements, including how you have used learning from other tasks to meet new demands

After you take a practice test, review how well you have done. Unfortunately, you don't get a chance to see which questions you answered incorrectly when you take the online test. If you can take note of the questions you are either having to guess or are not sure about as you answer them on screen, then you know which areas need further attention when you resume your learning.

The LP key skill asks that you to review your progress on at least two occasions. You can either do it after different practice tests or make one occasion after a practice test and the second occasion after the real thing.

You may find that by doing one of your reviews after the actual test you will have more to discuss. Pay particular attention to the official feedback from your DSA test. This will be useful evidence for your portfolio and will help you identify targets you have met or areas needing more attention.

What do you want to do next?

Context

At some point you may have to consider what your next move is to be in terms of the course or career you what to pursue. There is a wide range of opportunities and course choices available and as you decide on what opportunity to follow up you could be generating evidence for your PS key skill.

The key skill can support you through the often arduous process of identifying, investigating and selecting the most appropriate post-school or college option and can help you organise your efforts in a systematic and effective way. This guidance is based around suggestions about how to use the choices you have to make in terms of which course and higher education institution you choose to try to attend as one way of generating evidence for PS.

This type of opportunity may also be useful for generating LP evidence. It may also be possible to take a similar approach to finding employment.

Explore a complex problem, come up with three options for solving it and justify the option selected for taking forward

In a sense the 'complex problem' you will be addressing is what to do next, given the courses you are taking, the course or career you want to pursue and the places available. You need to start by establishing what help and support exists around you in the school or college. Consultation with teachers, careers advisers and parents will be a useful starting point as you investigate the range of opportunities available. Agree what it is you want to do and the alternatives you are prepared to consider. Aiming for a degree? Then familiarise yourself thoroughly with the Universities and Colleges Admissions Service (UCAS) procedures, literature and website. Identify helpful resources, e.g. UCAS handbooks, university and college prospectuses, student handbooks, careers guides, videos, CD-ROMs and websites. You can also identify when the open days are in your favoured higher education institutions. There will also be a range of careers and degree course conventions you could attend and telephone helplines to use. There is a comprehensive list of useful published information in the booklet titled *How to Apply* produced by UCAS.

UCAS has a website at **www.ucas.com**

You need to use all these sources of help and advice as a way to explore the problem and devise strategies to help you come up with a plan to help you eventually make a decision. You need to work out what your priorities are in terms of making your next move. It may be that location is the most important factor; perhaps the main deciding influence is who offers a particular course with location less of an issue. The type of course may be the most important. You might be keen to do work experience as part of the course or you may prefer courses where you specialise early or you can keep your options open and delay making specific choices until later in the course.

As well as academic matters make sure you consider the more personal matters and practical issues. Do you want to commute daily from home or move and live independently as a student? Weigh up the time and costs related to commuting and the financial implications of living away from home if you are at all unsure. Investigate the cost and availability of student accommodation in places that interest you and consider matters such as access to sport, entertainment and other recreation. Will there be people around that you know. Will you need to make new friends? You may even want to attend specific higher education institutions for the sporting or social facilities they offer.

You need to devise options to help you solve your problem from all of the questions you need to consider and sources of information and help available. Then you need to take one option forward. Your options need to centre on ways to eventually come up with a restricted range of courses you want to apply for, in institutions you are happy with, bearing in mind any other criteria you need to satisfy. This is your eventual solution. Then you can complete your UCAS forms and application process, confident that you have come up with choices that are both obtainable, given your current situation, and are desirable in terms of your own personal wishes and aspirations.

Keep a journal or diary to keep track of your work, the information you collect and the information you still need. Also use it to enter in dates of open days, conventions and, most importantly, deadlines for applications and other important timelines. After you have attended something (e.g. open day) make a brief entry about your thoughts on the usefulness of the event and what assistance it may have been in helping you reach your goal.

You will also need to:

- Be realistic in terms of where your current programme of study will take you
- Check out the likely entry requirements of potential courses
- Review your whole approach with a tutor, addressing your strategy in the light of your progress on your current course of study
- Find out as much as you can about grants, student loans, fees, equipment costs and factor this information into your researches
- Assess whether you need to practice for interviews, create a CV, prepare your National Record of Achievement, prepare a Personal Statement, strengthen your non-academic interests etc.

Remember it is not about just choosing a course; you need to select the right course for yourself at the most suitable establishment.

Having examined what is available you may also wish to consider other options. The attraction of a *gap year* working in a voluntary capacity, pursuing a particular interest may appeal or earning the money you may need to make future study more feasible.

Plan and implement at least one option for solving the problem, review progress and revise your approach as necessary

The option you take forward will probably be a plan of some sort that will help you narrow your choices and eventually come up with a few that best meet your criteria. So this section is about getting on with it and working through the plan, reviewing how you are doing in terms of getting closer to a solution as you go. Keep in regular contact with the appropriate careers or guidance people and use the people around you, e.g. parents, friends and teachers, to share your thoughts and discuss issues as you progress.

Consult your tutor and parents when finalising your options and pay particular attention to planning your Personal Statement.

Application for courses outwith the UCAS system can also be considered at this stage. Again follow the instructions and procedures laid down by the relevant institutions that interest you. Be prepared for interviews, keep a copy of any relevant CV, Personal Statement (UCAS) or any information of relevance to the particular courses you are interested in.

Consider constructing a flowchart to show all the steps, processes and decisions that will be involved in finding suitable courses. This will be a useful way to organise your thoughts of what needs to be done into some sort of logical sequence. You will clearly see where the key decision points are and it may help keep you focused on the task.

Apply agreed methods to check if the problem has been solved, describe the results and review your approach to problem solving

You need to ask yourself the following sorts of questions:

- Do you now have a range of options that suit your post-school or college ambitions? If not, then why not?
- Are they feasible?
- In the light of what you now know, is there anything that you might have done differently in selecting your course choices?
- What advice could you pass on to others?

You should be able to reapply your original criteria to your final list and use this as a way of helping you prioritise. This could be done as a way of reviewing your results and helping you draw conclusions about the appropriateness of your choices and your original criteria. Before you do this, re-evaluate your criteria for selecting courses, checking that they are still appropriate, making any changes as necessary.

An alternative approach would be to use the UCAS application process as the bulk of the PS3.2 activity, i.e. where you plan to implement one option for solving the problem. This means your initial efforts centre around making the choices needed and doing the preparation work necessary to complete the form. The final stage of the PS work focuses on the offer of places when they start to materialise. It will involve prioritising them and making informed decisions about which ones you will hold and which you will discard. The methods you use to make these informed decisions could be based around assessing those offers that best meet the original criteria you used to select courses. Start by establishing if your original criteria are still valid and assess if your opinion or position on any has changed. Again discussions with parents, tutors and friends will help.

You can make your final choices become part of the overall review of the progress you have made to date in terms of problem solving.

Index